Healing with Crystals Decoded for Women and Seniors: Improve Sleep, Rejuvenate Memory, and Alleviate Arthritis.

Contents

Healing with Crystals Decoded for Women and Seniors: Improve Sleep, Rejuvenate Memory, and Alleviate Arthritis. 1

    Introduction 3

    Chapter 1 3

        The Role of Intention in Crystal Healing 5

        Programming Crystals for Specific Needs 6

    Chapter 2: Embracing Nightly Tranquility: Crystals for Enhancing Sleep 7

        Understanding Insomnia in Seniors and How Crystals Can Help 7

        Top Crystals for Sleep and Their Properties 8

        Checklist for Creating a Sleep-Inducing Environment with Crystals 8

        Amethyst: The Tranquility Stone for Better Sleep 9

        How to Use Moonstone for New Beginnings in Sleep Patterns 9

        Lepidolite: The Stress-Relieving Sleep Aid 11

        Setting Up a Sleep-Inducing Crystal Grid in Your Bedroom 12

        Crystals Under Your Pillow: Do's and Don'ts 14

        The Connection Between Sleep, Crystals, and Lunar Cycles 15

        Sodalite: Harmonizing Mind and Body for Sleep 17

        Crafting a Personalized Crystal Sleep Amulet 18

    Chapter 3: Reviving Memory with Crystals 19

        Understanding Memory Loss and How Crystals Can Support 19

        Top Crystals for Memory Support 20

        Checklist for Creating a Memory-Boosting Crystal Kit 20

        Clear Quartz: Clarity for the Mind 21

        Using Fluorite to Enhance Focus and Clear Confusion 22

        Pyrite for Mental Stamina and Memory Support 23

- Developing a Daily Ritual with Crystals for Cognitive Health 24
- Tiger's Eye: The Stone of Mental Sharpness 26
- Crystals for Encouraging Neuroplasticity and Learning 27
- The Role of Meditation with Crystals in Memory Support 28
- Hematite: Grounding Thoughts for Better Focus 30
- Building Your Memory Support Crystal Kit 31

Chapter 4: Alleviating Arthritis with Crystal Energies 32
- The Energetic Approach to Understanding Arthritis 32
- Visualization Exercise: Crystal Meditation for Arthritis Relief 33
- Incorporating Crystals with Lifestyle Adjustments 34
- Copper: Conductivity for Pain Relief 34
- Green Aventurine: The Stone of Vitality and Growth 36
- Creating a Pain-Relief Crystal Grid for Arthritis 36
- Malachite: The Transformation Stone for Pain Management 38
- Turquoise: Strengthening the Physical Body 39
- Daily Practices: Incorporating Crystals into Your Pain Management Routine 40
- Blue Lace Agate: Soothing Inflammation and Encouraging Healing 41
- The Importance of Grounding to Alleviate Pain 42
- Crafting a Healing Crystal Pouch for Arthritis 43

Chapter 5 Integrating Crystals into Your Daily Routine 45
- Crystals in the Home: Creating Energetic Harmony 46
- Wearable Crystals: Jewelry and Accessories for Healing 47
- Crystals at Work: Enhancing Productivity and Focus 49
- Traveling with Crystals: Protection and Peace on the Go 50

Chapter 6: Tailoring Crystals to Healing to Senior Needs 52
- Enhancing Digestive Health with Crystals 53
- Crystals for Heart Health and Circulation 54
- Supporting Respiratory Health with Crystal Energy 55
- Crystals for Boosting Immune System in Seniors 56
- Managing Blood Pressure with Healing Stones 58
- Crystals for Emotional Well-being and Loneliness 59
- Enhancing Eye Health with Crystal Therapy 60
- Crystals for Skin Rejuvenation and Health 62

Conclusion 63

References 64

Introduction

Since my earliest memories, crystals have fascinated and comforted me, and I've enjoyed exploring them. My journey into the world of crystal healing started as a personal quest. I was searching for natural ways to enhance well-being, soothe the spirit, and navigate life's challenges. After years of studying, experimenting, and personal experience, I've witnessed the profound impact that these earth treasures can have on our health and happiness. I hold a deep connection and respect for the power of crystals, and it is from this place that I share my knowledge and passion with you.

This book is written to empower senior women with practical and accessible knowledge about crystal healing. It aims to address common health concerns such as sleep improvement, memory rejuvenation, and arthritis alleviation. Starting with the basics, we'll explore how crystals can be used to address specific ailments. I invite you to join me on a journey towards healing. Together, we will explore the world of crystal healing with an open heart and curiosity. This journey isn't just about physical health, but also about unlocking a more vibrant, healthy, and fulfilling phase of your life. Let's embrace the possibilities that await us. Welcome to a journey of discovery, healing, and profound personal growth.

Chapter 1

The fascination with crystals and gemstones dates to ancient civilizations. Even before modern medicine, people revered these treasures of the earth for their mystical properties. For example, the Egyptians used lapis lazuli for adornment and believed it offered spiritual protection and ensured a safe journey into the afterlife. They also used malachite as eye shadow, believing it had protective qualities against the evil eye. Similarly, the Greeks held crystals in high regard and attributed various powers to them.

The word 'crystal' comes from the Greek word 'krustallos', meaning frozen light, indicating their belief in the divine origin of these stones. They used amethyst to ward off intoxication, believing that it possessed calming energies. Moving East, the Chinese have used jade in their medicinal practices for centuries. Jade is a stone revered for its purported healing properties and is a symbol of purity, health, and spirituality.

Choosing Your First Crystal: A Beginner's Guide

Selecting your first crystal can be an exciting yet overwhelming process, given the vast array of options available. This guide aims to simplify this process, helping you to choose a crystal that resonates with you on a personal level.

Considerations for Selection

When you set out to pick your first crystal, think of it as an act of connecting. Consider the following factors to help you:

- **Intuition**: Often, the right crystal chooses you. Pay attention to the immediate pull or attraction you feel towards a particular stone. This intuitive choice can be a sign that the crystal's energy aligns well with your own.
- **Physical Appeal**: The color, shape, and texture of a crystal contribute to its appeal and can influence its effect on you. A visually appealing crystal can evoke feelings of happiness and contentment every time you see or touch it.
- **Specific Healing Needs**: Reflect on what you aim to achieve with crystal healing. Are you looking for emotional balance, physical healing, or spiritual growth? Identifying your needs can help narrow down your choices.

Understanding Crystal Properties

A brief introduction to some common crystals can help you make an informed choice:

- **Clear Quartz**: Known as a versatile healer, it's reputed to amplify energy and thought, making it ideal for a wide range of uses.
- **Amethyst**: Favored for its calming properties, it's excellent for reducing stress and promoting peaceful sleep.
- **Rose Quartz**: Symbolizing love and harmony, this crystal is believed to enhance relationships and encourage self-love.
- **Citrine**: Associated with prosperity and positivity, it can help to manifest your intentions and bring joy.
- **Black Tourmaline**: A powerful protector, it's recommended for those seeking to ward off negative energies and secure their space.

Sources for Purchasing Crystals

Finding a reputable source for your crystals is crucial to ensure their quality and authenticity. Here are some tips:

- **Local Crystal Shops**: These offer the advantage of physically experiencing crystals before purchase. Staff can also provide valuable advice and insights.
- **Gem Shows**: These events allow you to explore a wide variety of crystals from different vendors, often at competitive prices.
- **Online Stores**: Convenient but requires caution. Look for shops with positive reviews and clear, detailed photos of their products.
- **Estate Sales or Antique Shops**: Occasionally, you might find unique and powerful crystals here. It's essential to cleanse them thoroughly before use.

When selecting a crystal, inspect it for any chips or cracks that might affect its energy. Also, inquire about the crystal's origin and ensure it's been ethically sourced.

The Role of Intention in Crystal Healing

The idea of intention plays a crucial role in crystal healing by connecting our conscious desires with the natural energies of crystals. Our intentions help us direct and enhance these energies, aligning them with our own objectives for personal growth and healing. When our intentions are clear and positive, they can effectively resonate with the vibrational frequencies of the crystals, creating a powerful synergy that aids us in our pursuit of wellness.

Methods for Setting Intentions

Setting intentions with crystals involves a few thoughtful steps, each contributing to a deeper connection with the stone and a clearer focus on your desired outcomes. Here's a simple guide to get you started:

1. **Choose Your Crystal**: Let intuition guide you in selecting a crystal that resonates with your current needs or goals.
2. **Cleanse Your Crystal**: Before setting your intention, cleanse your crystal to clear any previous energies it may have absorbed. This can be done through smudging, soaking in salt water, or leaving it under moonlight.
3. **Find a Quiet Space**: Setting intentions is a meditative process. Find a quiet space where you can sit comfortably without distractions.
4. **Hold Your Crystal**: Take your cleansed crystal in your hands, closing your eyes to center your focus. Take deep breaths to ground yourself and calm your mind.
5. **Visualize Your Intention**: With a clear mind, visualize your intention. Imagine your goal as already achieved, focusing on the feelings this accomplishment brings. The more vivid your visualization, the stronger the intention.
6. **Affirm Your Intention**: While holding the crystal, state your intention aloud or in your mind. Use positive, present-tense affirmations like "I am healed," "I am protected," or "I attract abundance."
7. **Seal the Intention**: Conclude your intention-setting by expressing gratitude to the crystal for its support. You can do this by simply saying thank you aloud or in your mind.

Common Cleansing Methods

There are as many ways to cleanse crystals as there are types of crystals themselves. Here are a few widely used methods:

- **Moonlight**: The gentle, purifying energy of moonlight is ideal for cleansing most crystals. Simply place your crystals outside or on a windowsill during a full moon, allowing them to bask in the moon's glow overnight.
- **Sunlight**: Sunlight, with its vibrant and energizing qualities, can also cleanse and recharge your crystals. However, be mindful as prolonged exposure can fade some crystals. A few hours of morning sunlight are usually sufficient.
- **Water**: Running water can help wash away negative energies. Hold your crystal under a natural stream or tap water for a minute or so. Note, however, that not all crystals are water-friendly; some may dissolve or become damaged.

- **Smoke from Herbs**: Smudging, the practice of burning sacred herbs like sage or palo santo, is another effective way to cleanse crystals. Pass your crystals through the smoke to envelop them in the cleansing energy of the herbs.
- **Sound**: The vibrational energy of sound, produced by singing bowls, tuning forks, or even the human voice, can also clear and recharge crystals. The sound waves help to reset the crystal's vibrational frequency.

Frequency of Cleansing

How often you cleanse your crystals depends on several factors, including how regularly you use them and the types of energy they're exposed to. A good rule of thumb is to cleanse your crystals:

- After purchasing them to clear any energy from their previous handling.
- Before and after using them for healing work or setting intentions.
- Monthly, under the full moon, as a routine maintenance practice.

However, trust your intuition. If a crystal starts to feel dull or heavy, it may be time for cleansing, regardless of the schedule. Remember, regular cleansing ensures that your crystals remain vibrant conduits of energy, ready to support you in your healing journey.

Programming Crystals for Specific Needs

Imagine that your crystal is like a sponge that absorbs the emotional, physical, and spiritual energies that it comes across. This could include residual stress from a difficult day or the ambient energies from the environment. Just like a sponge can only absorb so much liquid before it needs to be wrung out, your crystal also needs regular cleansing to release these energies and recharge. This not only preserves the natural vibrational frequency of your crystal but also ensures that it is aligned with your current intentions and tuned to you.

Steps for programming crystals

The process of programming a crystal requires clarity, focus, and a few steps:

- **Choose Your Crystal Wisely**: Start by selecting a crystal that naturally resonates with the goal you have in mind. For instance, Citrine is often associated with abundance, making it a fitting choice for financial aspirations.
- **Cleanse Your Crystal**: Ensure your crystal is energetically clean before programming. This removes any previous programming or energy that may interfere with your intent.
- **Define Your Goal**: Clarity is key. Clearly articulate the specific outcome you're seeking. The more detailed, the better.
- **Hold and Connect**: Hold the crystal in your hand, close your eyes, and take a few deep breaths. Establish a connection with your crystal, feeling its energy merge with yours.
- **Program Your Crystal**: With your goal firmly in mind, visualize it as already achieved. Imagine this outcome traveling from your mind, down your arm, and into the crystal. You may also want to verbalize your goal, stating it aloud as you hold the crystal.

- **Seal the Programming**: Conclude the programming by expressing gratitude to the crystal for its assistance. Visualize a light surrounding the crystal, sealing in the programming.

Maintaining programmed crystals

Keeping your programmed crystals at their peak efficacy involves a couple of key practices:

- **Regular Cleansing**: Even though a crystal is programmed, it can still pick up extraneous energies. Regular cleansing ensures these don't muddy its programmed intent. How often you cleanse will depend on use and exposure to different environments.
- **Reprogramming**: As your goals evolve or once a goal is achieved, you may find it necessary to reprogram your crystal. This can be done following the same steps as the initial programming, ensuring your crystal's focus remains aligned with your current aspirations.
- **Respect and Care**: Treat your programmed crystals with respect and care. When not in use, store them in a place that honors their significance. This reinforces the energy and intent imbued within them.

Chapter 2: Embracing Nightly Tranquility: Crystals for Enhancing Sleep

During the night, when everything quiets down and the busyness of the day fades away, sleep becomes our refuge. However, for many people, especially seniors, achieving restful sleep is not an easy task. Insomnia often disrupts their pursuit of peaceful sleep. This is where crystals come in as not just silent companions but gentle guides that lead us back to the calming embrace of a good night's sleep. Their subtle energies, a guiding light in the darkness, whisper of both ancient wisdom and modern comfort, assuring us of a return to the rejuvenating power of deep, tranquil slumber.

Understanding Insomnia in Seniors and How Crystals Can Help

The Prevalence of Insomnia in Seniors

At night when the world quiets down and the day's rush fades away, sleep becomes our sanctuary. However, for many people, especially seniors, getting a good night's sleep is not easy. Often, the pursuit of peaceful sleep is disrupted by the restless dance of insomnia. In such situations, crystals can be more than just silent companions. They can act as gentle guides that lead us back to the peaceful embrace of sleep. Their subtle energies, a beacon in the night, whisper ancient wisdom and modern comfort, offering a return to the healing power of deep, restful slumber.

How Crystals Can Aid Sleep

Crystals may help alleviate insomnia by emitting a calming energy that counteracts the restless energy that keeps us awake. These crystals work like gentle hands, easing the tension in our minds and bodies and promoting a sense of relaxation that can lead to better sleep. These effects are not based on magic, but rather on the subtle influence of the crystals' vibrational energies on our bioenergetic field, which fosters harmony and encourages restful sleep.

Selecting the Right Crystals for Sleep

Selecting the right crystal for a good night's sleep is similar to choosing the perfect pillow. It should feel just right. It's advisable to look for crystals that have calming properties, such as Amethyst, which is known for its ability to soothe the mind and emotions, or Lepidolite, which contains lithium, a common ingredient in anxiety medication. The most important thing is to find a crystal whose energy aligns with your sleep needs and resonates with you.

Integrating Crystals into a Sleep Hygiene Routine

Incorporating crystals into your nightly routine is a simple yet effective way to promote better sleep. You can place them on your nightstand, under your pillow, or even create a small altar near your bed with crystals that are dedicated to sleep. As you prepare for bed, pick up your chosen crystal and hold it, allowing its energy to calm your mind and body. This ritual, repeated nightly, signals to your body and mind that it's time to wind down, creating a conducive atmosphere for deep, restorative sleep.

Top Crystals for Sleep and Their Properties

- **Amethyst**: Calms the mind, and eases anxiety.
- **Lepidolite**: Contains lithium and promotes deep relaxation.
- **Selenite**: Clears negative energy and induces peacefulness.
- **Moonstone**: Balances emotions and supports restful sleep cycles.

Checklist for Creating a Sleep-Inducing Environment with Crystals

- Select crystals based on their sleep-promoting properties.
- Cleanse your crystals regularly to maintain their energy.
- Place crystals strategically around your sleeping area.
- Develop a nightly routine that includes time with your crystals.
- Monitor your sleep patterns and adjust crystal placements as needed.

Incorporating crystals into your sleep routine is not just about placing stones around your bed. It's about creating a holistic environment that promotes sleep. From the gentle light of a selenite lamp to the calming weight of an amethyst under your pillow, every element of this crystal-infused sanctuary plays a role in easing your mind and body into sleep.

The goal is not just to fall asleep, but to rediscover the joy and rejuvenation that comes from deep, peaceful rest cradled in the gentle energies of the earth's gifts. Tonight, as you prepare for sleep, let your crystals guide you back to the tranquil depths of nightly rejuvenation where dreams are born, and the body finds its rest.

Amethyst: The Tranquility Stone for Better Sleep

The Amethyst stone has a beautiful purple hue, resembling the colors of a twilight sky. It has been revered across cultures and ages for its calming properties, providing a sense of tranquility. This stone is particularly useful in aiding restlessness and insomnia. Its beauty is not the only thing that captivates, but its ability to bring peace makes it an essential ally in the quest for a restful night.

Ways to Use Amethyst for Sleep

Incorporating Amethyst into your nighttime routine can be done in various intuitive and effective ways:

- **Beside the Bed**: A simple yet powerful placement. Positioning Amethyst on a bedside table allows its calming energies to permeate your sleep space, creating an aura of tranquility.
- **Under the Pillow**: For those who seek a more direct connection, placing a small Amethyst under the pillow can provide comforting energies throughout the night, promoting peaceful sleep.
- **Amethyst Geodes**: A larger Amethyst geodes in the bedroom not only serves as a stunning natural artifact but also acts as a reservoir of calming energies, beneficial for those particularly troubled by sleep disturbances.

Amethyst and Dream Work

Beyond its sleep-promoting properties, Amethyst also plays a significant role in the realm of dreams. It is said to:

- Enhance dream recall, allowing for a clearer memory of dreams which can be particularly beneficial for those who practice dream work as part of their spiritual practice.
- Support peaceful dream states, acting as a guardian against nightmares and ensuring that your journey through the dream world is one of discovery and serenity.

This dual role of Amethyst, as both protector and guide in the nocturnal realm, emphasizes its value not just for physical rest, but for emotional and spiritual rejuvenation.

How to Use Moonstone for New Beginnings in Sleep Patterns

Moonstone is a gem that shines with a subtle white and blue hue, reminiscent of the moon's glow. It is associated with lunar energy and represents the cyclical nature of the moon, which reflects the natural ebb and flow of our sleep patterns. Moonstone is not just a beautiful stone but has a profound ability to align our internal rhythms with the broader cycles of nature. As a

Resetting Sleep Patterns with Moonstone

For those grappling with insomnia or erratic sleep schedules, Moonstone offers a gentle but effective means of resetting internal clocks. Its calming energies soothe the mind, ease anxiety and restlessness that often bar the path to sleep. Here are some strategies for incorporating Moonstone into your sleep routine:

- Begin by holding a piece of Moonstone in your palm each night before bed. As you cradle this luminous stone, visualize its soft, lunar light enveloping you, guiding you toward a state of peaceful slumber.
- Place Moonstone on your bedside table or under your pillow as a physical reminder of your intent to embrace healthier sleep patterns. Its presence serves as a silent sentinel, warding off disturbances and fostering a serene sleep environment.

Moonstone Placement for Optimal Benefits

The placement of Moonstone within your sleeping environment can significantly amplify its benefits. Consider these locations:

- **Beside the Bed**: A Moonstone placed on a nightstand act as a beacon of calming energy, its soft luminescence reminiscent of moonlight streaming through a window.
- **Under the Pillow**: For a more intimate connection, a smaller piece of Moonstone can be tucked under the pillow, providing direct access to its tranquil energies throughout the night.
- **In a Sleep Amulet**: Crafting a sleep amulet with Moonstone and wearing it around your neck in the hours leading up to bedtime can help prepare your mind and body for rest.

Combining Moonstone with Other Rituals

To enhance the effects of Moonstone, consider integrating it with other sleep-promoting practices:

- **Lavender and Moonstone**: Pairing Moonstone with the soothing scent of lavender creates a powerful synergistic effect. Lavender's calming aroma, known for its sleep-inducing properties, complements the stone's tranquil energy. Place a few drops of lavender essential oil on a diffuser near your bed, alongside your Moonstone, to create a serene atmosphere conducive to sleep.
- **Meditation with Moonstone**: Engage in a brief meditation session with Moonstone before bedtime. Hold the stone in your hands or place it in front of you as you focus on your breath and the sensation of calm permeating your being. This ritual not only relaxes the mind but also deepens your connection with the stone's energy.
- **Moonstone and a Warm Bath**: Incorporate Moonstone into a pre-bedtime warm bath ritual. You can place Moonstone around the bathtub or wear your amulet to imbue the water with its calming essence. The combination of warm water and Moonstone's energy is a powerful precursor to a restful night.

Moonstone is more than just a gemstone, as it can be a helpful companion in achieving restful sleep. Its gentle and nurturing energy can be a source of hope for those who wish to improve their sleep patterns. Moonstone doesn't just provide comfort; it also offers a practical way to rejuvenate and heal. By incorporating Moonstone into your nightly routine, its luminescent energy can guide you towards the natural rhythms of rest and wakefulness, leading to peaceful nights and energetic days.

Lepidolite: The Stress-Relieving Sleep Aid

Lepidolite is a stone that emerges as a guardian of peace in the realm of slumber, where tranquility reigns supreme. It comes in hues ranging from lilac to soft pink and carries within it the rare gift of lithium, a natural mineral known for its calming effects. Lepidolite's unique composition endows it with remarkable stress-relieving capabilities, making it an invaluable ally for those nights when anxiety seeks to steal away sleep.

Lepidolite's Calming Properties

Lepidolite, a mineral containing lithium, is known for its soothing properties and is often used in anxiety medication. When held or placed nearby, Lepidolite interacts with our bioenergetic field, promoting a sense of calm and relaxation. It's as if the stone is gently whispering to the restless parts of ourselves, leading them towards serenity and preparing us for a peaceful night's sleep.

Using Lepidolite to Reduce Bedtime Anxiety

Incorporating Lepidolite into your evening routine can help create a peaceful environment for a good night's sleep. Here are some practical tips to help you harness its calming energy:

- **Place Lepidolite by Your Bedside**: A simple yet effective method. Having Lepidolite on your nightstand serves as a visual and energetic reminder to release the day's stresses.
- **Lepidolite Bath Ritual**: Create a pre-sleep ritual by adding Lepidolite to your bathwater. The water amplifies the stone's energies, while the warmth relaxes the body, preparing you for sleep.
- **Wear Lepidolite Jewelry**: Donning a piece of Lepidolite jewelry in the hours leading up to bedtime can help maintain a calm aura, gradually easing you into a state ready for sleep.

Lepidolite in Combination with Meditation

Meditation finds a powerful enhancer in Lepidolite. Together, they create a synergy that amplifies the benefits of both. Here's how to integrate Lepidolite into your meditation:

- **Hold or Place Lepidolite Near You**: Begin your meditation by holding Lepidolite in your hands or placing it in front of you. Its presence serves to deepen your meditative state, inviting a profound sense of peace.
- **Focus on the Stone's Energy**: As you meditate, visualize the calming energy of Lepidolite enveloping you. With each breath, imagine its soothing essence infusing your being, dispelling anxiety, and tension.
- **Post-Meditation Ritual**: Conclude your meditation by expressing gratitude to Lepidolite for its guidance. This not only seals the meditative practice but also strengthens your bond with the stone.

In the dance between night and day, where rest battles restlessness, Lepidolite stands as a beacon of tranquility. Its unique blend of natural lithium and serene energy offers a haven from the storm of anxiety, guiding us gently toward peaceful sleep. With its presence, we are reminded of the power of natural remedies and the importance of nurturing our minds and bodies to prepare for rest. So tonight, as the stars awaken and the world quiets, let Lepidolite be your guide. Allow it to lead you through the gates of sleep into a realm where dreams flourish and the body finds its much-needed repose.

Setting Up a Sleep-Inducing Crystal Grid in Your Bedroom

During the quiet hours before sleep, a carefully arranged crystal grid can be a powerful catalyst for deep and rejuvenating rest. This ancient practice combines the geometry of the grid with the vibrational energies of crystals to amplify intentions. The beauty of the crystal grid is not only in its aesthetic appeal, but also in its ability to create a calming and resonant field of energy, thereby transforming your bedroom into a sanctuary of serenity.

Basics of Crystal Grids

A crystal grid is a collection of crystals and stones arranged in a specific pattern, to focus and amplify energy towards a particular intention. This practice is based on the sacred geometry that underlies everything in the universe, from the patterns of galaxies to the intricate shapes of plants. By arranging crystals in patterns that mirror this fundamental geometry, we tap into a concentrated and harmonious energy flow, which enhances the individual power of each crystal to bring about the outcomes we desire.

Designing a Grid for Sleep

Creating a crystal grid for sleep involves several steps, each adding a layer of intention and energy to the final arrangement:

1. **Select a Location**: Your grid should ideally be placed where it can influence your sleep undisturbed. A bedside table or a shelf near your bed are perfect spots, ensuring the grid's energies envelop you as you rest.
2. **Choose a Pattern**: Start with a simple pattern, such as a spiral or flower of life. These patterns are not just visually calming but also resonate with the soothing, cyclic energies conducive to sleep.
3. **Prepare Your Space**: Cleanse the area where you'll set up your grid, either by smudging with sage or using sound vibrations from a bell or a singing bowl. This ensures a clean, energetic slate.

Selection of Crystals for the Grid

The crystals you choose should resonate with calming, sleep-promoting energies. Here's a harmonious combination to consider:

- **Center Stone**: A large piece of Amethyst, acting as the anchor for tranquility and protective energies.

- **Surrounding Stones**:
  - **Moonstone**: For its soothing lunar connection and support of restful sleep cycles.
  - **Sodalite**: To calm the mind and ease into a peaceful slumber.
  - **Rose Quartz**: Infusing the grid with gentle, loving energies conducive to sweet dreams.
  - **Clear Quartz Points**: Positioned outward around the perimeter, amplifying and directing the collective energy of the grid.

Activation and Maintenance of the Grid

By activating your grid, it transforms from static to vibrant.

- **Set Your Intention**: Hold a clear intention for restful sleep in your mind. You might find it helpful to write this down on a piece of paper, folding it beneath the center stone.
- **Activate the Grid**: Using a clear quartz point or your finger, trace the pattern of the grid, starting from the outside and moving towards the center stone. As you trace the pattern, envision a light connecting the crystals, charged with your intention for deep sleep.
- **Maintenance**: Your grid will need regular cleansing, especially if your sleep patterns begin to shift or if the energy in the room changes. Smudging with sage, placing selenite on the grid, or using sound cleansing can rejuvenate its energies. Additionally, reactivating the grid with your intention every full moon keeps it vibrant and potent.

Once activated, the sleep-inducing crystal grid becomes a powerful ally for achieving restful nights. The crystals are carefully selected and arranged according to the patterns of sacred geometry, creating a harmonious energy field that promotes deep, rejuvenating sleep. As the moon crosses the night sky and the world around you become silent, your crystal grid serves as a testament to your intention for peace and rest. It is a guardian of your sleep, ensuring you wake up feeling refreshed and energized.

Creating a Nighttime Crystal Ritual for Deep Rest

The hours leading up to bedtime are a special time when our bodies and minds prepare to rest. Establishing a nighttime routine can help signal to our systems that it's time to wind down and get ready for deep sleep. Crystals can be helpful allies during this time, as their energies can create a sense of calm that promotes relaxation and sleep.

Weaving Crystals into Your Nighttime Rituals

Integrating crystals into pre-sleep routines can enhance the ritual's effectiveness and infuse it with calming properties. Here are some ways to incorporate crystals into your nightly rituals:

- **Crystal-Infused Baths**: A warm bath before bed is a time-honored method of easing the body into a state of relaxation. Adding bath salts infused with calming crystals like Rose Quartz or Blue Calcite can amplify the water's soothing effects, turning your bath into a cocoon of serenity.

- **Meditation and Crystals**: A brief meditation session, with the aid of crystals like Howlite or Fluorite, can help quiet the mind's chatter, making it easier to slip into sleep. Hold a crystal in each hand or place it around you as you meditate, focusing on the flow of your breath and the tranquil energy emanating from the stones.
- **Journaling with Crystal Support**: For those whose minds are a whirlwind of thoughts at night, journaling can serve as an outlet, a way to download these thoughts onto paper. Keeping a piece of Sodalite or Lepidolite nearby as you journal can enhance mental clarity and emotional balance, making it easier to let go of the day's worries.

Crystals Renowned for Their Relaxing Properties

Integrating certain crystals into your nighttime routine can create a calm and restful environment, leading to better sleep.

- **Howlite**: Known for its soothing energy, Howlite can calm an overactive mind and ease insomnia. Its gentle vibration is particularly helpful in quieting thoughts and emotions, paving the way for a peaceful slumber.
- **Selenite**: This luminescent crystal is revered for its ability to clear negative energy and instill deep peace. Placing Selenite in your bedroom or holding it during meditation can create a serene atmosphere, ideal for restful sleep.
- **Angelite**: With its soft, angelic energy, Angelite promotes feelings of comfort and security. It's especially beneficial for those who experience nighttime anxiety or fear, enveloping them in a blanket of protective calm.

Crystals Under Your Pillow: Do's and Don'ts

The night brings quiet and darkness, which offers the promise of rest and rejuvenation through sleep. Many people use crystals to help them sleep by placing them under their pillow. This practice is very personal and can be applied in various ways. It works by using the energy of the crystal to connect with the mind of the dreamer. In this article, we explore the different ways of choosing and using crystals to enhance sleep, while prioritizing safety and comfort. These natural companions can provide a gentle power to help you sleep better.

Benefits of Sleeping with Crystals

Having crystals close by during sleep, under your pillow, creates an intimate energy exchange that can enhance the quality of rest. These benefits are multi-faceted:

- **Emotional Balance**: Certain crystals work to soothe the waters of emotional turmoil, ensuring a calm state of mind conducive to sleep.
- **Energetic Cleansing**: As we sleep, crystals can help to clear negative energy, promoting a restorative sleep environment.
- **Intuitive Connection**: Placing crystals under the pillow can deepen your connection to your subconscious, potentially enhancing dream clarity and recall.

Best and Worst Crystals for Under the Pillow

When selecting crystals for sleep, understanding their energetic properties is necessary. Here are some recommendations and cautions:

- **Recommended Crystals**:
    - **Amethyst**: Its calming energy is perfect for soothing the mind and warding off nightmares.
    - **Rose Quartz**: Known for its gentle, loving energy, it promotes peaceful dreams and emotional healing.
    - **Black Tourmaline**: Offers protection against negative energies, ensuring a safe space for rest.
- **Crystals to Avoid**:
    - **Citrine**: While positive, its energizing properties might be too stimulating for rest.
    - **Red Jasper**: Known for its grounding effect, it may also invigorate, making it challenging to wind down.
    - **Clear Quartz**: Although versatile, its amplifying energy can sometimes intensify thoughts or feelings, hindering sleep.

Safety and Comfort Considerations

While the benefits of sleeping with crystals are significant, safety and comfort are paramount:

- **Size and Shape**: Opt for smaller, smoother crystals to prevent discomfort or injury. Sharp edges or large stones could cause physical discomfort or even be dangerous if shifted during sleep.
- **Material Sensitivity**: Be aware of any allergic reactions to certain minerals or crystals. If you have sensitive skin, consider placing the crystal near your bed instead of directly under the pillow.
- **Emotional Reactions**: Pay attention to how you feel both before and after sleeping with a crystal. If you experience increased agitation or unsettling dreams, it may be best to choose a different crystal or place it further from your bed.

During the calm moments before sleep, many people find comfort in placing crystals under their pillow as a personal and meaningful practice. This allows for an exchange of energy, which can be nurturing to the soul and promote peaceful rest. By carefully selecting, preparing, and positioning these crystals, they become protectors of the night, ensuring a safe, comfortable, and rejuvenating slumber.

The Connection Between Sleep, Crystals, and Lunar Cycles

The moon's cycles have a significant impact on the natural world, including our sleep patterns and behaviors. As a celestial body, it mirrors the ebb and flow of our life cycles, from the energy of new beginnings to the quietude of reflection. The moon's sway over our nocturnal rest has been celebrated in traditional beliefs, guiding us towards crystals that resonate with lunar energy and help us harmonize our sleep. Nestled within the rhythmic dance of the cosmos, this cosmic interplay can be recognized and harnessed to improve our overall well-being.

Crystals Aligned with Lunar Energy

During the dance with the lunar phases, specific crystals become our natural allies, as their energies are in harmony with the moon's pull. These stones not only serve as tools for healing but also as conduits for the moon's serene essence, leading us toward peaceful and restful sleep.

- **Moonstone**: Aptly named, it embodies the moon's gentle strength, its energy fostering hormonal balance and soothing emotional turbulence that might disturb sleep.
- **Selenite**: Radiating pure lunar light, this crystal cleanses the sleep space of stagnant energies, inviting in vibrations that nurture deep, peaceful slumber.
- **Labradorite**: Known as the stone of magic, labradorite connects us to the mystical energy of the moon, enhancing intuition and protecting dream exploration.

Harmonizing Crystal Practices with Lunar Phases

To optimize the benefits of lunar crystals for sleep, align your practices with the moon's phases.

- **New Moon**: A time for setting intentions. Cleanse your sleep crystals under the dark sky, infusing them with your desires for restful nights ahead.
- **Waxing Moon**: As the moon grows, focus on building positive sleep habits. Incorporate moonstone into your nightly routine, its energy supporting the gradual enhancement of sleep quality.
- **Full Moon**: With energies at their peak, use this time to recharge your crystals, placing them where moonlight can touch them, revitalizing their potency for sleep support.
- **Waning Moon**: A period for release. Hold a piece of labradorite, meditating on letting go of sleep anxieties and disturbances, cleansing your path to peaceful rest.

Moon Rituals for Insomnia

Integrating lunar rituals with crystals can create a powerful synergy, aligning our sleep patterns with the natural world. These simple practices invite the moon's soothing energies into our nightly rest.

- **Lunar Bathing**: On nights graced by the moon's presence, hold your chosen sleep crystal close, stepping outside to bask in the moonlight. Allow its serene light to envelop you and your crystal, setting the stage for tranquil sleep.
- **Moonstone Water**: During the waxing to full moon phases, place a moonstone in a glass of water overnight, letting it charge with lunar energy. In the morning, use this water to anoint your forehead, temples, and heart, carrying the moon's calming essence with you into sleep.
- **Labradorite Dream Journaling**: Keep a labradorite stone and a journal by your bed. Before sleeping, hold the labradorite, setting the intention for clear, insightful dreams. Upon waking, jot down any dreams or feelings in your journal, exploring the messages revealed under the moon's influence.

Through the following practices, we incorporate the moon's cycles into our pursuit of peaceful sleep, allowing its rhythmic energy to guide us into nights filled with tranquility. The crystals, in their silent wisdom, serve as beacons of lunar light, harmonizing with our vibrations to promote sleep that rejuvenates and heals. Through this sacred alignment, we attain not only rest but also a deeper connection to the universe, cradled in the arms of the night sky, under the watchful gaze of the moon.

Sodalite: Harmonizing Mind and Body for Sleep

Sodalite is a gemstone that features rich, deep blue hues, interspersed with white calcite. Its appearance mirrors the tranquil vastness of the evening sky. This gemstone is highly revered for its ability to balance the conscious and subconscious mind. It serves as a bridge to peaceful sleep for those whose nights are often disrupted by an overactive mind. Sodalite's unique energy signature not only calms the mental chatter but also aligns the physical body with the restorative rhythms of the night.

Methods for Using Sodalite

To weave the energies of Sodalite into the fabric of your nighttime routine, consider these approaches:

- **Bedside Companion**: Place a piece of Sodalite on your nightstand. Its presence serves as a visual and energetic reminder to decompress and let go of the day's stresses as you prepare for sleep.
- **Pillow Placement**: For a more intimate connection, a small, polished piece of Sodalite can be slipped under the pillow. This allows for a direct resonance with its calming energies throughout the night, promoting deep and uninterrupted sleep.

Pairing Sodalite with Other Crystals

Pairing Sodalite with other crystals enhances its sleep-promoting qualities, creating a holistic energy blend for comprehensive sleep support.

- **Amethyst and Sodalite**: Combining Sodalite with Amethyst bridges the gap between mental calm and emotional tranquility. Amethyst's ability to soothe emotional turbulence complements Sodalite's mental clarity, together fostering an environment ripe for restful sleep.
- **Lepidolite and Sodalite**: Lepidolite, with its lithium content, brings a profound layer of relaxation to the mind and body. When paired with Sodalite, the duo acts to relieve both mental and physical tension, easing the journey into sleep.
- **Clear Quartz and Sodalite**: Clear Quartz, known as a master healer, amplifies the calming properties of Sodalite. This combination not only enhances Sodalite's effectiveness but also purifies the sleep space, creating a vibrational sanctuary for rest.

The interplay of Sodalite with complementary stones creates a tapestry of energies that surrounds the sleeper with peaceful vibrations. This harmonized state helps the mind and body achieve the equilibrium necessary for deep, restful sleep. Integrating Sodalite into your sleep routine can be a gentle yet effective way to ease the transition from wakefulness to sleep. Its calming blue hues, reminiscent of the night sky, serve as a constant reminder of the natural cycles of rest and activity that govern our lives. By aligning our internal rhythms with these cycles, Sodalite opens the door to nights that are filled with restful sleep and days that are imbued with clarity and calm. Through its presence, we are invited to explore the depths of our inner tranquility, finding in its soothing embrace a nightly refuge from the demands of the world.

Crafting a Personalized Crystal Sleep Amulet

The interplay of Sodalite with complementary stones creates a tapestry of energies that can help you experience deep, rejuvenating sleep. This harmonized state can help your mind and body find the equilibrium necessary for restful sleep. Incorporating Sodalite into your sleep routine offers a gentle and effective way to ease the transition from wakefulness to sleep. Its calming blue hues, reminiscent of the night sky, serve as a constant reminder of the natural cycles of rest and activity that govern our lives.

You can create a sleep amulet as a meaningful way to carry the comforting energies of crystals with you into the realm of dreams. This tangible piece of tranquility not only provides a physical touchstone to the serene energies conducive to rest but also acts as a focal point for your intentions, magnifying their presence in your nightly retreat.

Selecting Crystals for Your Amulet

Selecting the right crystals for your amulet is a highly individualized choice that depends on your specific sleep issues and preferences. Take some time to think about the areas where you want to enhance your sleep. Whether it is about falling asleep more quickly, having a more restful sleep, or being able to remember your dreams more vividly, some crystals can help. Here are some suggestions for crystals that may address your common sleep concerns:

- For easing into sleep: **Lepidolite**, with its gentle sedative properties, helps calm the mind and body.
- For deeper, uninterrupted sleep: **Amethyst** promotes a state of tranquility throughout the night.
- For dream work: **Moonstone** enhances connection to the subconscious, aiding in dream recall.

Creating Your Amulet

Assembling your sleep amulet is a process of intention. You will need:

- A small, soft pouch or a piece of cloth to hold your crystals.
- Selected crystals cleansed and ready for use.
- A piece of string or ribbon, if opting for a cloth wrap.

To assemble:

1. Place your cleansed crystals in the center of the pouch or cloth.

2. While doing so, focus on your intention for each stone, mentally imbuing them with your wishes for restful sleep.
3. If using a cloth, gather the corners and secure them with string or ribbon, creating a small bundle.
4. Finally, hold the completed amulet in your hands, reaffirming your sleep intentions, and visualize the amulet absorbing these desires, ready to manifest them in your nightly journey.

Using Your Amulet

Incorporating your amulet into your bedtime routine allows its energies to blend with your own, creating a peaceful atmosphere that is ideal for sleep. You may want to consider placing it under your pillow or on your nightstand, where its presence can gently influence your sleep environment. Others prefer to hold their amulet in their hands as they settle into bed, focusing on their breathing and the calm it brings.

In creating a personalized sleep amulet, you are not just making a simple accessory. You are forging a key that unlocks deeper, more restorative sleep. This amulet, infused with your intentions and the calming energies of chosen crystals, becomes a nightly companion that guides you toward a peaceful slumber. It serves as a constant reminder of the power within our intentions and the natural world's ability to bring them to life.

As we conclude our exploration of crystals for sleep, we are reminded of the gentle strength these precious earth treasures offer us in our pursuit of rest. From the calming depths of Amethyst to the soothing touch of Lepidolite and the protective shield of Black Tourmaline, each crystal carries the promise of peaceful nights and refreshing mornings.

Although this chapter is just one strand in the tapestry of our well-being, it weaves together ancient wisdom and personal intention, guiding us toward harmony with the natural rhythms of rest. As we continue on our journey, let the knowledge gained here serve as a foundation not only for improved sleep but also for a deeper connection with the supportive energies of the earth. The journey is ongoing, and each step will be enriched by the wisdom of the past and the personal discoveries that lie ahead.

Chapter 3: Reviving Memory with Crystals

Forgetting where you put your glasses is a common occurrence that makes us wonder about memory. It's not just about misplaced objects, but also the precious moments spent with loved ones, the laughter shared over a cup of coffee, or the wisdom gained from years of experience. Memory shapes who we are, and as we age, nurturing it becomes as important as tending to a cherished garden. Crystals, with their subtle energies, can offer a helping hand in this process, not as a miraculous solution, but as companions in maintaining cognitive vitality.

Understanding Memory Loss and How Crystals Can Support

Memory Loss in Aging

As we grow older, it's not uncommon to experience difficulties in remembering names or finding the right words. It's a natural part of the aging process, which affects our memory and cognitive functions. Scientists attribute this shift to various factors, including changes in the structure of the brain and the way neurons communicate. Despite its complexity, knowing that this change is common does not make it any less frustrating.

Selecting Crystals for Memory Support

Choosing crystals is a bit like picking out the right tool for a job. Each crystal has its unique properties:

- **Fluorite** is known for its ability to clear mental fog, making it a go-to for focus and clarity.
- **Hematite** offers grounding, which can be helpful when your thoughts feel scattered.
- **Amethyst** brings a sense of calm, reducing stress that can cloud thinking.

When selecting, hold the crystal in your hand. Notice how it feels, and trust your intuition. It's about finding a match that resonates with you.

Integrating Crystals into Cognitive Wellness Routines

Incorporating crystals into daily life can be simple and enjoyable. Here are a few suggestions:

- Keep a **Fluorite** stone on your desk to aid focus during tasks or hobbies that require concentration.
- Carry **Hematite** in your pocket on days filled with errands, as a grounding touchstone.
- Place **Amethyst** by your bedside to promote peaceful sleep, essential for memory consolidation.

Top Crystals for Memory Support

A guide to using crystals like Fluorite, Hematite, and Amethyst for cognitive health, presented in a colorful chart format.

Checklist for Creating a Memory-Boosting Crystal Kit

- Choose 3-5 crystals that resonate with you for focus, clarity, and calm.
- Cleanse your crystals regularly to maintain their vibrational energy.
- Keep a journal noting any changes in memory or cognitive function as you work with these crystals.
- Experiment with different placements and ways of carrying or wearing your crystals to find what works best for you.

In today's world, where multitasking is often praised, focusing on one thing at a time can be a game-changing practice. Crystals can serve as a gentle reminder of this practice, as their steady presence encourages a moment of pause, of breath, and of centering. In these moments, clarity blossoms, and memory - that intricate tapestry of our experiences - finds new strength. By simply choosing a crystal, carrying it with you, or placing it in your living space, you're taking a step towards supporting your cognitive health. It may seem like a small gesture, but it honors the wealth of memories you've accumulated and the many more you'll continue to create. In this way, crystals become more than just beautiful stones; their companions on the journey of remembering, of cherishing the moments that make life truly rich.

Clear Quartz: Clarity for the Mind

Clear Quartz is often referred to as the 'Master Healer' due to its versatility and strength, especially in mental enhancement. Its crystalline structure is not only visually appealing but also helps in promoting clarity of thought and improving memory retention. This transparent gemstone acts as a mirror, reflecting and amplifying our natural ability to concentrate and remember, making it an essential ally in our efforts to maintain a sharp and agile mind.

Properties of Clear Quartz

Using Clear Quartz for Memory Support

Clear Quartz is highly regarded for its ability to amplify energy and intention. This property is particularly beneficial for improving mental clarity and memory. Imagine a beam of light passing through a prism and emerging on the other side, not only intact but radiantly dispersed. In the same way, Clear Quartz magnifies our cognitive efforts and intentions, however faint they may be, thus helping us think more clearly and remember information better.

Integrating Clear Quartz into your daily life can be both a delightful ritual and a powerful tool for cognitive support:

- **Desk Buddy**: Place a piece of Clear Quartz where you study or work. Its presence can help in maintaining focus on tasks at hand, making learning and working not just productive but also more enjoyable.
- **Wearable Intentions**: Clear Quartz jewelry, such as necklaces or bracelets, keeps the crystal's amplifying energy close, assisting in clear thinking throughout the day.
- **Memory Corner**: Create a small, dedicated space in your home with Clear Quartz and other memory-supporting crystals. This spot can serve as a go-to for moments of reflection or mental work.

Combining Clear Quartz with Other Memory-Supporting Activities

To enhance the effectiveness of Clear Quartz in improving memory and focus, complementary activities can be incorporated for a more holistic approach.

- **Mindful Reading**: Allocate time for reading in a quiet space with Clear Quartz nearby. This practice not only improves focus but also aids in absorbing and retaining information.
- **Brain Games**: Engage in puzzles or brain teasers while keeping Clear Quartz within reach. The crystal's energy can enhance your problem-solving skills and cognitive agility.

- **Nature Walks**: Sometimes, a change of scenery is what the mind needs to clear up. Take Clear Quartz on a walk-in nature, allowing the natural setting and the crystal's energy to refresh your mind and spirit.
- **Learning a New Skill**: Whether it's a language, instrument, or craft, learning something new can significantly boost cognitive functions. Keeping Clear Quartz close during practice sessions can amplify your focus and rate of learning.

Clear Quartz is a stunning gemstone that possesses luminous clarity and powerful energy. It is a testament to the beauty and power of nature's gifts. This gemstone is known for its ability to enhance mental clarity and memory, and it goes beyond the physical, touching the very essence of our cognitive capabilities. Every glint of light that dances across its facets is an invitation to connect more deeply with our thoughts, to remember with greater ease, and to embrace the brilliance of a clear, focused mind. Through our daily interactions with this "Master Healer," we find not just a tool for cognitive enhancement but also a companion in our lifelong journey of learning and remembering.

Using Fluorite to Enhance Focus and Clear Confusion

With its stunning range of colors and remarkable ability to clear mental clutter, Fluorite is like a breath of fresh air for our cognitive processes. It doesn't just scatter the fog; it transforms it, revealing a clear path marked by enhanced focus and sharpness of thought.

Fluorite's Properties for Mental Clarity

Fluorite is a stunning crystal that possesses more than just its visual appeal. It has a profound connection with the complex workings of the mind. Think of each color of Fluorite as a note in a melodious symphony, working together to clear the clutter and enhance focus. This crystal is exceptionally adept at balancing energies, making it an indispensable aid for tasks that necessitate sustained mental effort and accuracy.

Practical Uses of Fluorite

Including Fluorite in learning, work, and creative spaces can enhance cognitive function. Here are some ways to incorporate Fluorite into your cognitive support system.

- **Study Buddy**: Placing a piece of Fluorite on your desk or study area can act as a focal point, helping to maintain concentration and absorb new information more efficiently.
- **Creative Muse**: For those engaged in creative endeavors, Fluorite can help in steering clear of mental blocks, ensuring a smooth flow of ideas.
- **Workplace Harmonizer**: In bustling work environments, a Fluorite crystal can contribute to a balanced atmosphere, fostering clear communication and effective collaboration.

Creating a Fluorite Focus Grid

A crystal grid is a tool that utilizes the collective energy of stones arranged in a particular geometric pattern to manifest a desired outcome. If you want to enhance your mental clarity and concentration, crafting a focus grid with Fluorite can be a powerful way to achieve this. Here's a step-by-step guide on how to create your Flourite Focus Grid:

- **Select Your Space**: Choose a quiet and comfortable area where you can set up your grid, preferably in your study or workspace.
- **Gather Your Crystals**: Alongside Fluorite, consider incorporating Clear Quartz to amplify Fluorite's properties, and Amethyst for its calming influence.
- **Arrange Your Grid**: Begin by placing a piece of Clear Quartz at the center of your grid as an amplifier. Surround it with pieces of Fluorite, forming a circle or another geometric shape that resonates with you. Add Amethyst at the outer edges to bring calm to the focused energy you're cultivating.
- **Activate Your Grid**: With intention, touch each crystal, starting from the center and moving outward, envisioning your goal of enhanced focus and mental clarity. You might visualize a beam of light connecting each stone, sealing the grid's purpose.

Pyrite for Mental Stamina and Memory Support

Often referred to as "Fool's Gold" for its deceiving shine, Pyrite's true value lies in its ability to energize the mind and enhance cognitive functions. This metallic stone, with its glimmering surfaces, acts as a mirror, reflecting our capacity for enduring focus and sharp intellect.

Incorporating Pyrite into Daily Routines

Integrating Pyrite into daily routines can transform how one approaches cognitive tasks, especially those demanding endurance and precision. Here are practical ways to invite Pyrite's energy into your cognitive landscape:

- Position Pyrite on your workspace where its presence can act as a constant source of mental invigoration.
- During periods of intense study or brainstorming, keep Pyrite close by, allowing its energy to fortify your focus.
- For tasks requiring detail-oriented attention, place Pyrite amongst your tools or on the relevant books and materials to infuse them with its clarity-enhancing qualities.

Pyrite as a Talisman for Learning

Incorporating Pyrite into our daily routine can make a significant difference in how we approach life. Carrying or wearing Pyrite serves as a tangible reminder of our commitment to cognitive growth and memory support. Whether it's a small piece tucked in a pocket during exams or a pendant worn over the heart, Pyrite acts as a talisman that reinforces our learning efforts through its steadfast energy. This physical connection not only brings Pyrite's benefits closer but also aligns our energy with it, creating a symbiotic relationship that nurtures our cognitive faculties.

- **To Carry**: A small, polished piece of Pyrite in your pocket allows for discreet yet powerful support.

- **To Wear**: Pyrite jewelry, such as bracelets or necklaces, keeps the stone's energy in your auric field, continuously offering its mental stamina-boosting benefits.

Pairing Pyrite with Affirmations for Cognitive Enhancement

When used alongside Pyrite, affirmations amplify the stone's capacity to support cognitive functions. By vocalizing positive statements focused on mental clarity, stamina, and memory, you weave a more robust fabric of intention that Pyrite can latch onto and magnify. Consider incorporating these affirmations into your daily practice with Pyrite:

- "With Pyrite's energy, my mind remains sharp and focused, effortlessly retaining and recalling information."
- "I am a vessel of endless creativity and intellect, continuously nourished by Pyrite's vibrant energy."
- "Each day, my ability to concentrate deepens, supported by the steadfast power of Pyrite."

The practice of combining Pyrite with affirmations creates a dynamic interplay between the stone and speech, connecting the Earth's natural resources with the power of human intention. This practice not only enhances the immediate environment but also strengthens the mind's inherent abilities, paving the way for a richer and more vibrant cognitive experience. In the daily dance of life, where the mind is required to perform a symphony of tasks, from the mundane to the complex, Pyrite acts as the conductor, ensuring each note of thought and memory is played with precision and clarity. Its presence is a testament to the natural world's ability to support our intellectual endeavors, offering a foundation upon which we can build stronger and more resilient cognitive structures. Through Pyrite, we discover not just a tool for mental enhancement, but a partner in the lifelong pursuit of knowledge and understanding.

Developing a Daily Ritual with Crystals for Cognitive Health

Establishing a daily ritual with crystals nurtures our memory and cognitive function with every deliberate action.

Importance of Daily Rituals

It serves as a grounding moment, allowing us to center ourselves, clear the mental clutter, and set the stage for a day marked by clarity and enhanced memory function. These moments, dedicated to nurturing our minds, become the pillars of our cognitive health.

Selecting Crystals for Your Ritual

In a world that moves ever acceleratingly, carving out time for a daily ritual becomes a sacred practice, a declaration of self-care amidst daily responsibilities. This ritual is not merely an addition to our routines but a transformative process that can significantly impact our cognitive health. The first step in crafting your daily ritual begins with selecting crystals that resonate with your specific mental goals. This selection process is deeply personal, reflecting your intentions and the areas you wish to enhance or support. Consider the following as you choose your crystals:

- For memory enhancement, **Fluorite** offers a spectrum of support, its myriad colors mirroring the complexity of our cognitive processes.
- **Carnelian** ignites a spark of creativity and motivation, perfect for those seeking to invigorate their problem-solving skills.
- **Blue Lace Agate** brings a calming presence, ideal for those moments when stress threatens to overshadow clarity.

As you select your crystals, pay attention to how they feel in your hands and the immediate response in your body or intuition. This intuitive selection ensures that the crystals you incorporate into your ritual align with your cognitive and emotional landscape.

Creating Your Cognitive Health Ritual

Crafting a ritual that supports cognitive health involves a few simple yet profound steps. This ritual can be as brief or extensive as your schedule allows, but consistency is critical. Here's a suggested framework for a daily cognitive health ritual with crystals:

- Begin by finding a quiet space where you can sit comfortably without distractions. This space becomes your sanctuary for mental rejuvenation.
- Hold your selected crystal or crystals in your hands, closing your eyes as you take several deep, grounding breaths. With each inhale and exhale, envision clarity and focus infusing your mind, dispelling any fog or fatigue.
- Set an intention for the day related to your cognitive health. It could be as specific as wanting to remember all items on your to-do list or as broad as seeking overall mental clarity.
- Conclude your ritual by placing your crystals in a location where they'll be in your presence throughout the day, such as on your desk, around your neck, or in your pocket.

When practiced regularly, this ritual becomes a cornerstone of your daily routine, a moment dedicated entirely to nurturing your cognitive health and enhancing your memory.

Adapting Rituals as Cognitive Needs Evolve

Our cognitive needs and challenges are not static; they evolve with time, circumstances, and as we age. As such, it's essential to remain flexible and open to adjusting your daily ritual to meet these changing needs. Here are a few suggestions for evolving your ritual:

- Periodically reassess the crystals you're using. As your cognitive goals shift, different crystals may become more relevant to your needs. Introducing new crystals into your ritual can reinvigorate your practice and provide targeted support for your current challenges.

- Experiment with the timing of your ritual. While morning may be ideal for setting intentions for the day, an evening ritual can help in reflecting on the day's events, processing learnings, and releasing any mental burdens before sleep.
- Incorporate additional elements that support cognitive health, such as aromatherapy with essential oils known for their mental clarity benefits, like rosemary or peppermint. Pairing these with your crystal ritual can amplify the cognitive benefits.

As you continue to engage with your daily ritual, remember that its true power lies in the intention and attention you bring to each moment. Crystals are tools and partners in your journey toward enhanced cognitive health and memory. They serve as tangible reminders of your commitment to nurturing your mind, offering their vibrational support to help you navigate the complexities of life with clarity, focus, and an ever-sharp memory. This practice, woven into the fabric of your daily life, becomes not just a ritual but a pathway to a more vibrant, cognitively rich existence.

Tiger's Eye: The Stone of Mental Sharpness

Maintaining a sharp focus and a clear path toward problem-solving can sometimes feel like navigating through a dense fog in a world brimming with distractions and endless information streams. Here, Tiger's Eye emerges as a beacon of light, its rich, golden hues and protective energy providing clarity and a boost in confidence when faced with cognitive challenges. This remarkable gemstone, with its silky luster, mirrors the dynamic nature of our thought processes, encouraging adaptability and resilience.

Tiger's Eye for Focus and Problem-Solving

Tiger's Eye is a gemstone known for its grounding energy. However, it is also valued for its ability to boost mental clarity, sharpen focus, and improve problem-solving skills. The stone's vibrational energy promotes a balance between creative and practical thinking by harmonizing the yin and yang in our cognitive processes. This balance is critical for tackling complicated tasks or making decisions that require innovative thinking and logical deduction.

Methods for Using Tiger's Eye

Integrating Tiger's Eye into work or study environments can significantly amplify its cognitive benefits. Here are a few practical approaches:

- **Desk Placement**: Positioning Tiger's Eye on your desk or workspace acts as a constant source of focused energy, keeping you anchored and attentive to the task at hand.
- **Wearable Focus**: Incorporating Tiger's Eye into jewelry, such as bracelets or pendants, ensures that its clarifying energy remains within your auric field, enhancing mental stamina and sharpness throughout the day.
- **Study Sessions**: During study sessions, holding a piece of Tiger's Eye or placing it in clear view can help maintain a high level of concentration, making the absorption of new information more efficient.

Tiger's Eye and Challenging Cognitive Tasks

Tiger's Eye is best put to the test during times of intense mental exertion and cognitive challenges. This stone's energy helps to heighten awareness and sharpen perception, making it easier to focus on the key elements of a problem and eliminate distractions. When faced with moments that require quick thinking or decisive action, Tiger's Eye not only offers mental clarity but also provides the courage needed to make tough decisions.

- When faced with a complex issue, try holding a piece of Tiger's Eye, allowing its energy to fill you with confidence and clarity. Visualize the problem unraveling before you, with each strand being neatly sorted and addressed.

Incorporating Tiger's Eye into your daily routine can have a significant impact on your ability to focus and solve problems. Its grounded yet stimulating energy promotes a state of mental agility, allowing ideas to flow freely and solutions to emerge with clarity. Whether you're dealing with the complexities of work, study, or personal projects, Tiger's Eye can be a reliable ally, guiding you towards cognitive clarity and success. With Tiger's Eye by your side, every challenge can become an opportunity to sharpen your mind and illuminate the path ahead.

Crystals for Encouraging Neuroplasticity and Learning

The human brain, an intricate landscape of neural pathways and synaptic connections, is not a static entity but a dynamic one capable of remarkable transformation and growth. This ability, known as neuroplasticity, allows the brain to adapt, learn new skills, and recover from injuries by forming new connections. It is the foundation upon which all learning and memory-building rest, a testament to our potential for growth regardless of age.

Crystals, with their unique vibrational frequencies, can support this incredible capacity of our brains to rewire and enhance learning. While it may seem far-fetched to some, the energetic support provided by specific crystals can create an environment conducive to mental agility and cognitive flexibility.

- **Lapis Lazuli**, with its deep celestial blue, is often associated with wisdom and truth. It is believed to stimulate the intellect and enhance the desire for knowledge, making it an ideal companion for those engaging in academic pursuits or learning new skills.
- **Carnelian** ignites a fire of motivation and endurance. It's particularly useful for those moments when perseverance is needed, as in mastering a challenging subject or skill.
- **Malachite**, known for its rich green hues and intricate patterns, is considered a stone of transformation. It encourages risk-taking and change, which are essential components of neuroplasticity and learning.

Incorporating these crystals into your learning practices can be both a symbolic and energetic aid in your quest for knowledge and mental expansion.

- Place **Lapis Lazuli** on your study desk or wear it as a pendant during learning sessions to invite clarity and insight.

- Keep **Carnelian** nearby or hold it in your hand when you're working on mastering a new skill or subject. Its energizing vibrations can help maintain focus and determination.
- Meditate with **Malachite** before embarking on any learning journey that requires you to step out of your comfort zone. Its transformative energy can help ease the transition, making learning an exciting adventure rather than a daunting task.

Pairing these crystal practices with brain exercises to foster neuroplasticity can amplify the benefits and enhance cognitive abilities.

- **Memory Games**: Engage in memory exercises or apps designed to improve short and long-term memory. Keeping a piece of **Lapis Lazuli** nearby can enhance focus and information retention during these activities.
- **Creative Hobbies**: Activities such as drawing, painting, or playing a musical instrument stimulate different areas of the brain, promoting neuroplasticity. **Carnelian** can be a source of inspiration and creativity, encouraging artistic expression.
- **Language Learning**: Taking up a new language challenges the brain in unique ways, strengthening cognitive flexibility. **Malachite** can support this process by bolstering confidence and the willingness to make mistakes—a key part of learning.
- **Physical Exercise**: Physical activity is known to support brain health and encourage the formation of new neural connections. Incorporate small, wearable crystals like **Carnelian** in your workout gear to carry their energizing properties with you as you exercise.

Integrating crystals into your learning and brain exercise routines supports your cognitive functions and serves as a tangible reminder of your commitment to personal growth and mental agility. While the journey of learning and adapting is inherently subjective, the energetic companionship provided by these crystals offers a universal source of support, encouraging the brain's natural capacity for change and development.

The Role of Meditation with Crystals in Memory Support

When adorned with the subtle energies of crystals, the serene practice of meditation unfolds as a powerful tapestry for nurturing cognitive health and bolstering memory. This ancient art, deeply rooted in the quest for inner peace and clarity, finds a harmonious ally in crystals, each resonating with specific frequencies that support the mind's capacity for recall and focus.

Meditation for Cognitive Health

Meditation is a pause, a moment taken from the rush of daily life. This pause, though quiet, is profoundly active in its impact on cognitive health. Regular meditation has increased gray matter in the brain, particularly in areas associated with memory, stress regulation, and empathy. Focusing attention, whether on breath, a mantra, or a crystal, trains the brain in the art of concentration, enhancing memory and sharpening mental clarity.

Selecting Crystals for Meditation

Choosing the right crystals for meditation can feel like selecting the perfect spice to complete a dish, each one bringing its unique flavor to the experience. For memory and cognitive support, consider these crystalline companions:

- **Clear Quartz**: Revered for its amplifying properties, it enhances the intentions set during meditation, focusing the mind.
- **Blue Apatite**: Known to stimulate thoughts and ideas, it's beneficial for creative problem-solving and intellectual growth.
- **Green Jade**: Often associated with wisdom and balance, it aids in making insightful decisions and retaining information.

When selecting, let intuition guide you. The crystal that catches your eye or feels right in your hand is likely the one your cognitive self is drawn to.

Guided Meditation with Crystals

To incorporate crystals' supportive energies into your meditation practice, follow this simple guided meditation, which aims to enhance memory and focus.

1. Begin by finding a comfortable seated position, holding your chosen crystal in your hands. Let your eyes close gently.
2. Take three deep breaths, inhaling peace and clarity, exhaling any tension or clutter from your mind.
3. Visualize the energy of the crystal, a luminous aura that surrounds and permeates you, its light focusing your mind, sharpening your thoughts.
4. Silently affirm, "With each breath, my mind becomes clearer, my memory sharper. I am open to the wisdom within and around me."
5. Continue to breathe deeply, letting the crystal's energy infuse your being, enhancing your cognitive health with every inhale.
6. When you feel ready, slowly open your eyes, carrying the crystal's energy and the clarity it brings with you into the day.

Creating a Meditation Space with Crystals

Dedicating a space for meditation adorned with crystals creates a sanctuary for cognitive rejuvenation, a physical manifestation of your commitment to mental health. Here's how to make this sacred space:

- **Location**: Choose a quiet corner that feels comfortable and inviting. It could be a part of your bedroom, living room, or any area that can be dedicated to stillness.
- **Crystals**: Arrange your selected crystals around your meditation spot. You might create a small altar with Clear Quartz at the center to amplify the energies of surrounding stones like Blue Apatite and Green Jade.
- **Comfort**: Ensure your meditation space is comfortable. A cushion for seating, a soft mat, or a blanket can make the space inviting and conducive to prolonged periods of meditation.

- **Personal Touch**: Add elements that make the space uniquely yours. It could be a photograph of a place you find calming, a book of meditations, or a journal for capturing insights post-meditation.

This dedicated meditation space, enriched with crystal energies, becomes a haven for cognitive care. It stands as a testament to the power of stillness and the profound impact that moments of quiet reflection can have on our mental clarity and memory. In this space, with crystals as your guide, meditation unfolds as a practice and a pathway to a sharper, more vibrant mind. Here, in the tranquility of your sanctuary, cognitive health is nurtured, memories are cherished, and the mind is refreshed.

Hematite: Grounding Thoughts for Better Focus

In the quiet corners of our minds, where thoughts flutter and dance with the day's worries, finding focus can sometimes feel like trying to catch smoke with our bare hands. In these moments of mental flutter, Hematite shines as a beacon of stability. Known for its rich, metallic luster, Hematite is more than just a stone; it's a mental anchor, drawing the chaotic energy of an overactive mind down into the solid earth, grounding us in the present.

Hematite's Grounding Properties

Imagine, if you will, the feeling of your feet firmly planted on the ground after a dizzying spin. That sudden sense of stability, the world no longer whirling, is akin to Hematite's influence on the mind. This dense and cool-to-the-touch stone acts as a grounding rod, channeling excess mental energy away, allowing thoughts to settle and focus to sharpen. This unique property makes Hematite invaluable for memory retention and cognitive tasks, transforming mental scatter into structured thought.

Using Hematite During Work or Study

Incorporating Hematite into your work or study environment doesn't require grand gestures; simple actions often yield the most significant results. Here are a few ways to integrate Hematite into these spaces:

- Place a Hematite stone alongside your workstation or within your study area. Its presence alone can serve as a steady pulse of grounding energy, subtly enhancing your focus.
- Consider a Hematite paperweight. Not only does it serve a practical purpose, but it also anchors your workspace energetically, keeping your thoughts aligned and organized.
- For those who thrive on tactile connection, keeping a small piece of Hematite in your pocket allows for direct contact. A gentle touch or squeeze can serve as a grounding reminder, pulling your focus back when it starts to wander.

Hematite and Stress Reduction

Stress, the silent thief of mental clarity, often goes unnoticed until our minds are clouded, our thoughts tangled. Hematite addresses this intruder not by force but through grounding, dissipating the build-up of stress and anxiety that can hinder cognitive functions and memory. Its calming influence on the emotional body indirectly supports our mental faculties, ensuring our minds remain clear, focused, and ready to retain information. This serene state, fostered by Hematite, is where true cognitive well-being begins.

Pairing Hematite with Grounding Exercises

To fully embrace Hematite's grounding benefits, pairing it with physical grounding exercises can enhance its effect on cognitive well-being. These exercises, simple yet profound, reconnect us with the present moment, further amplifying Hematite's stabilizing properties:

- **Barefoot Grounding**: Whenever possible, stand or walk barefoot on the earth, be it grass, sand, or soil. Holding Hematite during this practice deepens the connection, aligning your energetic body with the earth's stabilizing forces.
- **Focused Breathing**: Sit quietly with Hematite in hand, focusing on deep, slow breaths. With each inhale, envision drawing in calm and focus; with each exhale, imagine releasing mental chaos and stress.
- **Visualization**: Close your eyes and visualize roots extending from your base, reaching deep into the earth, anchored by the weight of Hematite. Feel the exchange of energy, the stone drawing down excess thoughts, leaving you centered and calm.

Integrating Hematite into your daily routine through these exercises enhances your immediate environment and fortifies your mental resilience. This practice, over time, cultivates a space where focus thrives, where thoughts are no longer fleeting but grounded, ready to be channeled into productive, creative, and organizational efforts.

In the dance of daily life, where our minds are asked to juggle countless tasks and emotions, Hematite offers a moment of pause, a grounding touchstone amidst the whirlwind. Its rich and stabilizing energy transforms our approach to cognitive tasks, from work to study to creative endeavors. With Hematite as our ally, we find our thoughts no longer scattered but aligned, our focus sharpened, and our memory capacity enhanced. In its silent, steadfast way, this stone reminds us of the power of grounding, of the clarity found in stillness, and the strength that lies in focused intention. Through Hematite, we rediscover the art of concentration, the beauty of a mind at rest yet fully awake, attuned to the task at hand, and open to the vast potential.

Building Your Memory Support Crystal Kit

Each crystal brings unique energy and properties to the mix, offering a holistic approach to fostering memory and cognitive functions.

Essential Crystals for Memory Support

In assembling our cognitive toolkit, we consider a variety of crystals known for their ability to aid memory and bolster mental clarity. Here's a concise list of essential stones, each with its unique benefits:

- **Blue Kyanite**: Known for its alignment properties, it bridges gaps in communication between different aspects of cognition, fostering better recall and understanding.
- **Chrysocolla**: This stone calms the mind and eases fear, creating a peaceful state from which learning, and memory retrieval can easily occur.
- **Rhodonite**: It nurtures love and compassion, including self-compassion for our learning and memory processes, encouraging patience in our cognitive development.
- **Agate**: Offers grounding and analytical capabilities, promoting clear thinking and problem-solving, essential for effective memory function.

Assembling Your Crystal Kit

The process of putting together your memory support kit is both personal and intuitive. Start by selecting crystals you feel drawn to or those whose properties directly align with your cognitive goals. It's not about the number of crystals but their relevance and resonance with you. Here are steps to guide you:

- Begin by cleansing each crystal to reset its energy. This can be done using sage smoke, sound vibrations, or moonlight.
- Next, dedicate a pouch or box for your crystals, creating a physical home for your toolkit that's easily accessible.
- Arrange your crystals in the pouch or box, possibly categorizing them based on their specific uses or simply placing them in a way that feels right to you.

As we close this chapter, we understand that enhancing memory and cognitive function is a holistic journey. It encompasses the physical aspects of brain health and the energetic support we can harness through crystals. This journey is ongoing, a continuous exploration of how we can support our minds to be as vibrant and straightforward as possible. With our crystal kit in hand, we step forward, ready to engage with the world in a way that honors our cognitive health and cherishes our memory capacity.

Chapter 4: Alleviating Arthritis with Crystal Energies

Arthritis isn't just about the physical symptoms we feel; it's deeply intertwined with the energetic imbalances within us. Like a river overflowing its banks causing disruption, energy imbalances in our bodies can manifest as physical ailments, including arthritis. This perspective opens a new avenue for understanding and addressing arthritis, one that considers the body and the energy flowing within it.

The Energetic Approach to Understanding Arthritis

Holistic View of Arthritis

Viewing arthritis through a holistic lens allows us to see it as more than wear and tear or an inevitable part of aging. It's a signal, a sign that our body's energy isn't flowing as it should. It may be stagnant in some areas or overly turbulent in others. This imbalance can lead to inflammation, pain, and discomfort of arthritis.

Role of Crystals in Energy Balance

Crystals have been used for centuries to restore balance and harmony. Each crystal vibrates at its unique frequency, and these vibrations can interact with the body's energy field. For arthritis relief, crystals that promote energy flow, reduce inflammation, and soothe pain can be particularly beneficial. For instance:

- **Amethyst** helps in soothing inflammation and purifying the body's energy field.
- **Black Tourmaline** is known for its ability to ground and protect, helping to dissipate negative energy that could exacerbate arthritis symptoms.
- **Blue Lace Agate** offers calming and healing vibrations, easing stress and reducing the conditions that lead to inflammatory responses.

Complementary to Traditional Treatments

While the energetic approach offers a new perspective on managing arthritis, it's important to remember that crystal healing is meant to complement, not replace, conventional medical treatments. Consulting healthcare professionals, adhering to prescribed medicines, and incorporating crystals can create a well-rounded approach to managing arthritis.

Starting with Intention

Healing begins with intention. When using crystals for arthritis relief, setting a clear intention amplifies their efficacy. It could be as simple as holding a crystal and mentally affirming your desire for reduced pain and increased mobility. This intention sets the stage for healing, directing the crystal's energy towards your specific needs.

Visualization Exercise: Crystal Meditation for Arthritis Relief

Here's a simple exercise to incorporate crystals into your arthritis management routine:

1. Find a quiet, comfortable space where you can sit or lie down without disturbance.
2. Hold a crystal associated with healing arthritis, such as Amethyst, in your hand or place it on a nearby surface.
3. Close your eyes and take deep, steady breaths, allowing your body to relax.
4. Visualize the crystal's energy as a soothing light, enveloping the areas affected by arthritis. Imagine this light gently dissolving any blockages, easing pain, and restoring mobility.
5. Spend a few minutes in this visualization, then slowly open your eyes and return to your surroundings.

Real-life Application: Daily Incorporation of Crystals

Incorporating crystals into your daily life for arthritis relief can be seamless and practical. Keep a piece of Amethyst in your pocket or wear it as jewelry. Place Black Tourmaline near your workspace or living area to continuously benefit from its grounding energy. Before bed, place Blue Lace Agate under your pillow or on your nightstand to promote healing sleep.

Textual Element: Checklist for Choosing Arthritis Healing Crystals

- Look for crystals associated with reducing inflammation (e.g., Amethyst, Turquoise).
- Consider crystals that promote energy flow and alleviate pain (e.g., Garnet, Malachite).
- Choose crystals that resonate with you personally; you might be drawn to a particular one for reasons unique to your energy needs.
- Cleanse and program your crystals with your intention for healing and relief from arthritis.

Incorporating Crystals with Lifestyle Adjustments

For a holistic approach to managing arthritis, combine crystal healing with lifestyle adjustments:

- **Diet**: Incorporate anti-inflammatory foods like turmeric, ginger, and omega-3-rich fish. Place a crystal-like Amethyst or Turquoise in your dining area to remind you of your healing intentions.
- **Exercise**: Gentle, low-impact activities such as walking or swimming can improve joint mobility. Carry a small Garnet or Black Tourmaline for motivation and protection.
- **Stress Management**: Stress can exacerbate arthritis symptoms. Practices like yoga, meditation, and deep breathing, enhanced with the calming energy of Blue Lace Agate or Rose Quartz, can help manage stress levels.

Arthritis, with its myriad challenges, might seem like a relentless foe. Still, relief and healing are within reach through the harmonious balance of traditional treatments, lifestyle adjustments, and the subtle power of crystals. Just as a gardener tends to their soil with care and attention, we can also nurture our bodies, finding solace in the earth's gifts and regaining the joy of movement and ease.

Copper: Conductivity for Pain Relief

In natural healing, copper stands out for its unique ability to interact with our body's electrical system. This reddish-brown metal, familiar to us in everything from ancient jewelry to modern plumbing, possesses properties beyond its physical uses. Its conductivity, which makes it invaluable in wires and circuits, also plays a pivotal role in alleviating the discomfort and inflammation associated with arthritis.

Copper's Conductive Properties

Copper's ability to transfer energy efficiently isn't just a benefit in electronic devices and within the human body. Our bodies generate an electrical charge essential for the functioning of our nervous system and the movement of muscles. Copper interacts with this biological electricity, potentially helping to rebalance the body's energy and reduce the blockages that can lead to pain. This interaction is believed to facilitate the healing process, making copper an ally against the inflammation of arthritis.

- **Energy Flow**: Copper aids in maintaining the natural flow of energy within the body, which can be disrupted by arthritis.
- **Anti-Inflammatory**: Though scientific studies offer varying results, anecdotal evidence suggests copper's interaction with the body might reduce inflammation.

Wearing Copper for Arthritis

The tradition of wearing copper bracelets and rings for joint pain relief spans centuries, bridging cultures across the globe. This practice, rooted in historical anecdotes and folklore, has grown in popularity as people search for natural remedies to complement medical treatments for arthritis.

- **Skin Absorption**: Some proponents believe that wearing copper allows trace amounts to be absorbed through the skin, directly aiding affected joints.
- **Magnetic Therapy**: Modern copper bracelets often incorporate magnets, believed to further enhance copper's pain-relieving properties.

Combining Copper with Crystals

For those seeking to amplify copper's arthritis-relieving properties, pairing it with specific crystals can create a synergistic effect. Crystals, with their unique vibrational energies, can complement copper's conductivity, enhancing the body's natural healing processes.

- **Malachite**: With its deep green color and renowned healing properties, malachite works well with copper to soothe joint discomfort.
- **Turquoise**: Known for its anti-inflammatory effects, turquoise combined with copper can offer a double dose of healing energy.
- **Clear Quartz**: Can amplify copper's conductivity, potentially making it more effective in pain relief.

To integrate copper and crystals into a cohesive pain-relief strategy, consider the following:

- **Wear Together**: A copper bracelet adorned with healing crystals combines both elements in direct contact with the skin.
- **Place Nearby**: Keeping copper and chosen crystals near your resting area can create an ambient field of healing energy.
- **Meditation**: Holding copper and a crystal during meditation focuses intention on healing, enhancing energetic interaction.

In exploring the intersection of ancient wisdom and modern practices, copper is a timeless ally in the fight against arthritis. Its conductive properties and the energetic support of specific crystals offer a holistic approach to managing pain and inflammation. This blend of elements, grounded in the natural world, echoes the harmony we seek in our bodies—a balance of energy, relief from pain, and a return to ease of movement. Through mindful selection and care of copper and crystals, we tap into a wellspring of healing potential, opening ourselves to nature's gentle yet powerful support.

Green Aventurine: The Stone of Vitality and Growth

Green Aventurine, renowned for its soothing embrace and invigorating energy, emerges as a guardian for those navigating the discomforts of arthritis. With properties that echo the vitality of spring's first bloom, it offers a natural remedy to foster an environment where healing flourishes.

Soothing and Anti-Inflammatory Properties

With its gentle caress, Green Aventurine carries the essence of earth's healing energy. Its core resonates with soothing vibrations that extend a calming influence over the body, particularly beneficial for inflamed joints and tissues afflicted by arthritis. This tranquil stone, rich in silicates, mirrors the anti-inflammatory qualities of the lush greenery from which it draws its color, providing relief and comfort to aching limbs and weary spirits.

- Direct Application: For targeted relief, placing Green Aventurine directly on swollen joints can help alleviate discomfort. The stone's cool touch and healing vibrations work together to reduce inflammation and soothe pain.
- Environmental Harmony: Introducing Green Aventurine into living spaces not only infuses them with a serene ambiance but also continuously radiates its healing energy, aiding in the overall well-being of those within.

Support for Emotional Well-being

Arthritis, with its persistent pain, can cast long shadows over one's emotional landscape, often leading to feelings of frustration and limitation. Green Aventurine, however, with its uplifting energy, acts as a beacon of hope, its light piercing through the gloom to uplift spirits. This stone encourages a positive outlook, reminding those affected that the possibility for growth and renewal lies beyond the clouds of discomfort.

- Emotional Resilience: Carrying Green Aventurine as a personal talisman can bolster emotional strength, offering comfort during challenging times and reminding one of their inner resilience.
- Heart Chakra Connection: By resonating with the Heart Chakra, this stone fosters a sense of compassion—both for oneself and others—easing the emotional burden arthritis can impose.

Green Aventurine, in its essence, is a testament to the interconnectedness of body, mind, and spirit. It serves not merely as a stone but as a companion on the path to wellness, offering its healing touch to soothe physical discomfort while nurturing the emotional resilience necessary to bloom anew. Through its gentle guidance, those touched by arthritis can find solace and strength, embracing each day with renewed vigor and a heart open to the journey of healing.

Creating a Pain-Relief Crystal Grid for Arthritis

In the realm of crystal healing, the concept of a crystal grid represents a powerful synergy between geometry, intention, and the earth's gemstones. Think of a crystal grid as a mosaic, each piece placed with precision and purpose, working together to draw out a specific energy or outcome. When aligned towards alleviating arthritis pain, these grids become focal points of healing energies, tailored to soothe inflammation and ease discomfort.

Introduction to Crystal Grids

At its core, a crystal grid is an arrangement of crystals selected and placed in a geometric pattern to amplify their collective energies towards a set intention. This pattern acts as a conduit, harmonizing the vibrations of the individual crystals into a single, potent force. The beauty of crystal grids lies in their versatility; they can be configured to support a wide range of intentions, from attracting abundance to fostering love. In arthritis, the grid aims to target pain relief and reduce inflammation, creating a sanctuary of healing energy.

Designing a Grid for Arthritis Pain Relief

Crafting a crystal grid for arthritis involves careful consideration of both the crystals involved and their arrangement. Here's a step-by-step guide to creating your own pain-relief grid:

1. **Select Your Crystals**: Begin with a central stone that anchors your intention. Malachite, known for its potent pain-relieving properties, serves well as the centerpiece. Surround it with supporting stones like Amethyst for inflammation, Blue Lace Agate for soothing calm, and Clear Quartz to amplify the grid's overall energy.
2. **Choose Your Pattern**: The geometry of your grid can be as simple or complex as you wish. A basic circle, representing wholeness and continuous energy flow, is a good starting point. For more intricate energy work, the Flower of Life pattern, symbolizing creation, and unity, can be particularly effective.
3. **Prepare Your Space**: Before laying out your grid, cleanse the area and your crystals. Smudging with sage or palo santo clears old energies, setting a clean slate for your healing work.
4. **Lay Out Your Grid**: Begin by placing your central stone, then arrange your supporting crystals in your chosen pattern. As you place each stone, hold your intention for pain relief and healing in your mind, infusing the grid with your desire for wellness.

Activation and Maintenance of the Grid

With your grid laid out, activating it breathes life into your intention, setting the energies in motion:

1. **Activate With Intention**: Using a Clear Quartz point or simply your finger, trace the pattern of your grid, starting from the central stone and moving outward. As you trace, visualize a bright light connecting the stones, sealing the grid with your intention for arthritis relief.
2. **Maintain Your Grid**: Keep your grid in a place where it won't be disturbed, allowing it to continuously radiate healing energy. Re-activate it weekly, or whenever you feel the need, to keep its energy vibrant and focused on your healing.

Personal Stories of Relief

The potency of a pain-relief crystal grid is not merely theoretical but is echoed in the experiences of those who've found solace in its energies. Consider the story of Elena, who, after years of battling with rheumatoid arthritis, turned to crystal healing as a complementary therapy. Frustrated with persistent pain and unwilling to rely solely on medication, she crafted a crystal grid with Malachite at its heart, surrounded by Amethyst, Blue Lace Agate, and several Clear Quartz points. Within weeks of setting up her grid, Elena noticed significantly reduced flare-ups. The constant ache in her joints softened, allowing her more mobility and less reliance on pain medication. She attributes this improvement not just to the physical presence of the crystals but to the shift in her mental state, finding a renewed sense of hope and positivity that she believes has been crucial in her journey toward wellness.

Malachite: The Transformation Stone for Pain Management

In the lush expanse of the natural world, where rejuvenation and growth unfold with each season, a stone is as vibrant and renewing as spring itself. With its rich, verdant stripes, Malachite mirrors the essence of life's unending cycle of renewal. Within its depths, a force for profound transformation and healing vibrates, offering solace and relief to those navigating the challenges of arthritis. This stone, revered for millennia, holds the key to alleviating physical discomfort and nurturing the emotional resilience needed to thrive.

Malachite's Pain-Relieving Properties

Malachite, a carbonate mineral, is celebrated for its remarkable ability to ease pain and reduce inflammation. Its energy, deeply connected to the earth, acts as a balm, soothing aching joints and weary muscles. The stone's unique composition allows it to absorb negative energies, including the pain and stiffness associated with arthritis, transforming discomfort into a sense of relief. This process is akin to the earth absorbing the rain, turning it into nourishment for growth.

- To use Malachite for pain relief, consider placing the stone directly on areas affected by arthritis. Contact facilitates the transfer of healing energies, offering localized relief.
- For broader impact, carrying Malachite as a touchstone throughout the day allows its energy to continuously interact with your body's own, gradually easing discomfort and promoting mobility.

Practical Application of Malachite

Incorporating Malachite into daily routines unfolds as a practice of intention and mindfulness. Here are a few suggestions to seamlessly integrate this transformation stone into your life:

- **Wear Malachite Jewelry**: Bracelets, rings, or pendants not only bring Malachite's healing properties close but also serve as a constant reminder of your commitment to self-care.
- **Place in Sleeping Areas**: Positioning Malachite near your bed or under your pillow can help alleviate pain during rest, ensuring a more peaceful and rejuvenating sleep.

Emotional Support with Malachite

Beyond its physical benefits, Malachite offers a wellspring of emotional support. Arthritis, with its limitations, can often lead to feelings of frustration, sadness, or isolation. Malachite, resonating with the heart chakra, encourages positive energy flow, fostering emotional balance and resilience.

- **Meditation and Reflection**: Holding or meditating with Malachite can help release emotional blockages, making space for positivity and growth.
- **Journaling**: Keeping a journal and reflecting on your experiences while holding Malachite encourages emotional processing and healing.

Malachite stands as a testament to the healing power of nature, its verdant hues a mirror to the earth's boundless capacity for renewal. For those affected by arthritis, this stone offers physical relief and a path to emotional well-being, transforming the journey into one of resilience and hope. Its energy, rooted in the natural world's rhythms, provides a steady foundation to find balance, manage pain, and embrace each day with renewed strength. Through mindful application, care, and reflection, Malachite becomes more than a mineral; it transforms into a source of support, a beacon of healing in the journey toward wellness.

Turquoise: Strengthening the Physical Body

Turquoise, a gemstone as old as time, carries the essence of the skies and waters of our planet. Its healing virtues extend beyond its beauty, deeply ingrained in the lore of civilizations past and present. For those navigating the challenges of arthritis, Turquoise emerges as a guardian stone, enhancing physical strength and the immune system and offering a protective embrace that shields the body from further ailment.

Turquoise has long been revered for its life-affirming qualities. Depending on its copper and iron content, this magnificent stone, with its hues ranging from sky blue to lush green, acts as a holistic tonic for the body. It's believed to not only fortify the physical body but also to invigorate the immune system. This bolstering of bodily defenses is crucial for individuals dealing with arthritis, as it aids in reducing inflammation and minimizing the occurrence of flare-ups.

Wearing Turquoise, especially in forms that keep the stone in close contact with the skin, is a tradition. This direct contact allows the body to absorb the stone's healing vibrations, providing joint support and easing the discomfort that often accompanies arthritis. Turquoise bracelets encircling the wrist or rings adorning the fingers can serve as constant sources of healing energy, directly targeting areas afflicted by arthritis.

Integrating Turquoise with Healing Modalities

To create a holistic approach to managing arthritis, combining Turquoise with other healing practices can amplify its benefits. These complementary modalities work in concert with Turquoise, creating a multidimensional healing experience.

- **Acupuncture and Turquoise**: Acupuncture, a practice aimed at unblocking energy within the body, works harmoniously with Turquoise. The stone's energy can enhance the flow achieved through acupuncture, promoting faster relief from pain and stiffness.
- **Yoga and Turquoise**: Incorporating Turquoise into a gentle yoga practice can help focus the mind and body on healing. Placing Turquoise stones on your yoga mat as visual and energetic focal points can enhance the practice's joint-strengthening and flexibility-enhancing benefits.
- **Aromatherapy and Turquoise**: Using essential oils known for their anti-inflammatory properties, such as frankincense and lavender, in conjunction with Turquoise can create a soothing environment that supports healing on multiple levels.

Turquoise stands as a testament to the healing power of nature. It serves as a tool for physical healing and a symbol of the earth's boundless capacity to nurture and rejuvenate. For those who walk the path of arthritis management, Turquoise offers a shield against pain and a beacon of hope, reminding us that strength, protection, and healing are within reach. Through mindful integration with other healing practices and a commitment to ethical stewardship, this ancient stone can be a steadfast ally, empowering us to lead a life marked by vitality and grace.

Daily Practices: Incorporating Crystals into Your Pain Management Routine

In the soft light of dawn, as the world stirs awake, the ritual of integrating crystals into your day begins. This practice, a gentle weave of ancient wisdom into modern living, offers a foundation for managing arthritis pain through the harmonious energy of crystals. From the first moments of the morning to the quiet of the evening, crystals can become steady companions, their presence a subtle but constant source of relief and comfort.

Morning Rituals with Crystals

- **Greet the Day with Sunstone**: Begin each morning by holding a piece of Sunstone, a crystal known for its warm, energizing properties, which can stimulate the body's healing processes and alleviate morning stiffness. As you hold the stone, visualize the day ahead flowing with ease and your movements being fluid and free from pain.

Incorporating Crystals into Physical Therapy and Exercises

- **Enhanced Physical Therapy Sessions**: Bring a small pouch of crystals, such as Fluorite and Hematite, to your physical therapy appointments. These stones can lay nearby, lending their energy for increased focus and strength during your exercises.
- **Yoga and Stretching**: Place crystals around your yoga mat to create a circle of energy. As you move through your poses or stretches, imagine the crystals' energy supporting your joints, enhancing flexibility, and easing any discomfort.

Meditation and Visualization with Crystals

- **Focused Pain Relief Visualization**: Hold a piece of Lapis Lazuli or Turquoise during meditation. These stones are particularly adept at soothing inflammation and promoting

physical healing. Visualize their energy penetrating the areas of discomfort in your body, washing away pain and restoring health.
- **Evening Wind-Down**: As night falls, engage in a quiet meditation with Moonstone, which supports the body's natural healing rhythms and helps ease nighttime pain. This practice can help relax both mind and body, preparing you for a restful sleep.

This structured yet flexible routine of incorporating crystals into daily life for pain management embraces the full spectrum of their potential. From the tranquility of morning meditations to the reflective quiet of evening journaling, crystals offer a steady stream of support, weaving their healing energies into the fabric of everyday life. Their presence is a gentle reminder of the body's capacity for healing and the profound connection between the Earth's gifts and our well-being. As days flow into nights and seasons, shift, this practice becomes a personal testament to the power of crystals in navigating the challenges of arthritis, transforming each step into a stride toward balance, health, and harmony.

Blue Lace Agate: Soothing Inflammation and Encouraging Healing

Blue Lace Agate, with its gentle energy, is particularly beneficial for those grappling with arthritis discomfort. It is believed to possess anti-inflammatory properties, soothing the body's flare-ups and easing the tension that often accompanies chronic conditions. Furthermore, this stone promotes the flow of lymphatic fluids, which is essential in reducing swelling and enhancing the healing process.

- **Direct Contact**: For targeted relief, placing Blue Lace Agate directly on swollen joints can provide immediate comfort. The coolness of the stone, combined with its healing vibrations, works to diminish inflammation and soothe pain.
- **Wearable Relief**: Incorporating Blue Lace Agate into jewelry, such as bracelets or pendants, allows its healing energy to remain in close contact with the body throughout the day, offering continuous support.

Methods for Using Blue Lace Agate

Integrating Blue Lace Agate into daily life offers a simple yet effective means of harnessing its soothing energies. The stone's presence not only combats physical symptoms but also enhances the spaces it occupies, promoting a peaceful and healing environment.

- **Healing Spaces**: Placing Blue Lace Agate in areas where relaxation and rest occur, such as bedrooms or living rooms, infuses these environments with its calming energy, creating havens of tranquility.
- **Bath Companions**: Adding Blue Lace Agate to bathwater, perhaps in a mesh bag to keep them safe, turns a simple bath into a soothing ritual, where water and crystal energy combine to relieve arthritis discomfort.

Blue Lace Agate for Emotional Tranquility

Arthritis, with its chronic nature, can take a toll on the body, mind, and spirit. Blue Lace Agate addresses this holistic need, offering support that transcends physical healing. By fostering emotional tranquility, this stone helps mitigate the stress and frustration that often accompany arthritis, reinforcing the undeniable link between emotional well-being and physical health.

- **Meditative Companion**: Holding Blue Lace Agate during meditation can deepen the practice, guiding the mind to a state of peace and acceptance, which in turn can positively impact physical symptoms.
- **Support Circle**: Sharing Blue Lace Agate with friends or family members who also experience arthritis or other chronic conditions fosters a sense of communal support and understanding.

In the nurturing embrace of Blue Lace Agate, those who face the daily challenges of arthritis can find a gentle ally. With its soothing bands of blue and white, this stone offers a tangible connection to the calming energies of the earth and sky. Its presence in daily life, whether worn on the body, placed within living spaces, or used in healing rituals, brings peace and well-being. Through careful use and maintenance, Blue Lace Agate becomes a steadfast companion in the journey toward holistic health, proving that even in the face of chronic conditions, tranquility and healing are within reach.

The Importance of Grounding to Alleviate Pain

Within the earth's embrace lies a profound yet often overlooked remedy for the discomforts accompanying arthritis. This remedy is grounding, also known as earthing, which reconnects our body to the earth's natural energy. By its very nature, grounding encourages the flow of the earth's negatively charged ions into the body, which has been suggested to reduce inflammation and pain perception. Imagine the world as a giant battery that continuously replenishes us with vital, healing energy. By connecting to this source, we tap into a wellspring of health benefits, potentially easing the chronic pain of arthritis.

Crystals for Grounding

Amidst the myriad of crystals, specific stones stand out for their grounding properties, acting as conduits for the earth's healing energy. Hematite and Smoky Quartz are particularly noted for their ability to anchor us to the earth's core, offering stability and balance.

- **Hematite**, with its metallic sheen, reflects the strength and solidity of the earth. It's renowned for its grounding effects, helping to draw down pain and disperse negative energy.
- **Smoky Quartz**, ranging in color from light smoke to deep brown, acts like a filter. It absorbs harmful energies, including the discomfort of arthritis, and replaces them with a grounded calm.

Using these crystals in your arthritis management strategy can help align your body's energy with the earth's, fostering a sense of balance and well-being.

Grounding Exercises with Crystals

To enhance the benefits of grounding crystals, integrating simple exercises into your daily routine can amplify their pain-relieving properties. Here are a few practices to consider:

- **Barefoot Walking**: Whenever possible, walk barefoot on natural surfaces like grass, sand, or soil. Carry Hematite or Smoky Quartz in your pockets to deepen the connection to the earth's energy.
- **Crystal Meditation**: Sit or lie down outside, placing grounding crystals on or around your body, particularly near the base of your spine. Visualize roots extending from your body into the earth, anchoring you deeply into its calming presence.

Incorporating Nature into Healing

For a holistic approach to managing arthritis pain, merging natural grounding practices with crystal therapy offers a pathway to enhanced wellness. Here are some suggestions to weave the healing powers of nature with the stabilizing energy of grounding crystals:

- **Nature Walks with Crystals**: Take walks in natural settings, carrying or wearing grounding crystals. The combination of physical activity, connection to nature, and the crystals' energies can synergistically reduce pain and inflammation.
- **Outdoor Crystal Grids**: Create a small crystal grid in your garden or a natural space, using grounding crystals like Hematite and Smoky Quartz. This not only anchors the healing energies in the area but also serves as a focus for meditation or relaxation outdoors.
- **Sleeping Under the Stars**: Whenever possible, spend a night sleeping outside, placing grounding crystals around your sleeping area. The direct contact with the earth, combined with the crystals' energies, can promote a deep, healing rest.

Through the practice of grounding, we find a natural and accessible way to alleviate arthritis pain. By connecting to the earth, we open ourselves to its balancing energies, finding relief and stability. Grounding crystals like Hematite and Smokey Quartz serve as vital tools in this process, deepening our connection to the planet and enhancing the therapeutic effects. When combined with the inherent healing power of nature, these practices offer a promising avenue for managing arthritis pain, providing a foundation of well-being that supports both body and spirit.

Crafting a Healing Crystal Pouch for Arthritis

In the quiet moments of creation, where intention meets the tangible, crafting a healing crystal pouch emerges as a profoundly personal ritual. This small, portable haven for your chosen crystals serves not only as a physical reminder of your commitment to alleviating arthritis pain but also as a vessel for the concentrated energies of the earth's treasures. Through thoughtful selection and assembly, your healing pouch becomes a companion, offering continuous support and comfort as you move through your day.

Selecting Crystals for Your Pouch

The initial step in creating your healing pouch involves carefully selecting crystals. This process is akin to gathering allies with unique properties to aid in your quest for relief and well-being. When choosing crystals, consider their reputed abilities to address arthritis pain and inflammation, but also pay attention to your intuitive pull towards specific stones. Your connection to the crystals enhances their effectiveness, making them true partners in healing.

- **Aquamarine** for its soothing, cooling properties, reminiscent of clear, calm waters, can reduce inflammation and calm the mind.
- **Bloodstone** for its revitalizing energy, encouraging circulation and detoxification, which can be beneficial in managing arthritis symptoms.
- **Carnelian** for its warmth and stimulating properties, fostering a sense of renewed vitality and energy in the joints.

Creating Your Pouch

The creation of your healing pouch is a moment of intentionality, where every choice from the material to the color carries significance.

- **Materials**: Choose natural fabrics such as cotton, silk, or hemp. These materials honor the earth's elements and add an additional layer of natural energy to your healing pouch.
- **Colors**: Choose colors that resonate with healing and comfort. Blues and greens can reflect soothing and anti-inflammatory intentions, while reds and oranges might symbolize warmth and revitalization.
- **Symbolic Items**: Adding a small token, a piece of driftwood, a shell, or a handwritten affirmation can personalize your pouch further, imbuing it with a story, your story.

Using Your Healing Pouch

With your pouch crafted and crystals carefully nestled inside, it transforms into a source of ongoing support.

- Keep it close throughout the day, in a pocket or purse, allowing the crystals' energies to envelop you in a continuous healing embrace.
- At moments when pain flares or discomfort arises, hold the pouch in your hands, drawing comfort from its contents and the intentions they represent.
- Before sleep, place it under your pillow or on your nightstand as a guardian through the night, promoting restful sleep and healing.

In crafting a healing crystal pouch for arthritis, you weave together threads of intention, natural energy, and personal resonance, creating a tapestry of support that accompanies you through the day. This simple yet profound pouch serves as a reminder of your strength, resilience, and the natural allies that walk with you on the path to wellness. It's a testament to the power of the earth's gifts and the comfort they can provide.

Chapter 5 Integrating Crystals into Your Daily Routine

Imagine the gentle warmth of the morning sun caressing your face, a new day's promise mingling with the fresh scent of dew-kissed earth. This moment, ripe with potential, is your canvas, and crystals, with their vibrant energies, are your palette. Just as a gardener tenderly plants seeds, nurturing them to bloom, so too can you cultivate a routine that intertwines the grounding and uplifting powers of crystals into the fabric of your day.

In the soft glow of dawn, when the world whispers of quiet beginnings, there is an opportunity to infuse your day with intention and grace through crystals' subtle yet profound influence. From the moment you open your eyes to the tranquil stillness of the night, crystals can be your companions, offering support, focus, and a constant reminder of your connection to the natural world.

Setting intentions with crystals

Each morning, choose a crystal that resonates with the day's goals or how you wish to feel. Hold it, close your eyes, and take a deep breath. Visualize your intention, whether it's to face challenges with courage, find joy in small moments, or approach the day calmly. Whisper your intention to your crystal, then carry it as a tangible reminder of your inner resolve.

Crystals in morning meditation and yoga

Introduce crystals into your morning meditation or yoga practice to deepen your focus and grounding. Place a Clear Quartz crystal before you to amplify your intention, or hold a piece of Amethyst to invite tranquility into your practice. Let these moments with your crystals bridge the peace of your inner world and the bustling activity of the day ahead.

- **Visual Element**: A photo of a serene meditation space with crystals placed thoughtfully around a yoga mat, capturing the early morning light.

Dressing with crystal jewelry

Selecting crystal jewelry as part of your morning routine is an act of adornment and a powerful means of carrying your intentions with you. Choose a piece of jewelry with Lapis Lazuli for honest communication on a day filled with meetings, or wear a Black Tourmaline for protection during your commute. Let these pieces be accessories, guardians, and allies as you navigate the day.

By weaving these practices into the tapestry of your morning, you lay a foundation of mindfulness, intention, and connection. Crystals, with their enduring energies and beauty, serve as anchors, keeping you grounded in your essence amidst the whirlwind of daily life. They remind us that every day is a new opportunity to align our actions with our deepest values and aspirations, and in doing so, we transform ordinary moments into a rich, vibrant life.

Crystals in the Home: Creating Energetic Harmony

The subtle energies of crystals can weave a tapestry of harmony and protection in your home's sanctuary. It isn't just about placing stones randomly but about a mindful arrangement that aligns with your living space's natural flow, enhancing its vibrancy and making it a bastion against the chaos of the outside world.

Strategic Placement for Harmony

The art of positioning crystals throughout your home is akin to setting up invisible threads of energy that connect and balance the space. For example:

- **Entrance**: A welcoming Amethyst in the foyer dissolves stress, inviting calmness into your home right from the threshold.
- **Living Areas**: Citrine placed in living spaces fosters gatherings filled with laughter and good conversation, its sunny energy dispelling any lingering shadows.
- **Study or Workspace**: A cluster of Fluorite on your desk or bookshelf not only enhances focus and clears mental fog but also turns the area into a vortex of creativity.

Crystals for Protecting the Home

Your home deserves guardians at its gates, warding off anything that might disrupt its peace.

- **Black Tourmaline**: Positioning this stone near your home's entrances acts as a powerful shield, absorbing negative energies and ensuring they never make their way into your personal space.
- **Selenite**: Placing Selenite in windowsills fills your home with divine light, creating an angelic barrier that promotes purity and peace.

Enhancing Sleep Spaces

The bedroom, a realm of dreams and rest, benefits immensely from the serene presence of crystals.

- **Rose Quartz**: A Rose Quartz by your bedside infuses the room with loving energy, facilitating emotional healing as you sleep.
- **Moonstone**: Tucked under your pillow, Moonstone invites lucid dreams and helps you tap into your intuition, making your sleep both restful and enlightening.
- **Visual Element**: An infographic titled "Crystals for a Serene Sleep Space" illustrating the best crystals for enhancing sleep, their properties, and suggested placement in the bedroom.

Creating a Dedicated Crystal Space

Beyond scattering crystals throughout your home, dedicating a specific area to your crystal collection can create a focal energy point. This doesn't have to be elaborate; a simple shelf, a corner of a room, or a small table can serve as your altar. Here, you can:

- Gather crystals that resonate with your current intentions, creating a dynamic space that evolves with your needs.
- Incorporate elements of nature like plants or water features, enhancing the connection between your crystals and the natural world.
- Use this space for meditation, reflection, or as a retreat when you need to recharge, surrounded by your crystal companions.

This dedicated space becomes more than just a physical location; it's a portal to tranquility, a personal sanctuary where the mundane meets the magical.

- **Textual Element**: A step-by-step guide on creating your crystal altar, including selecting the location, choosing your crystals, and consecrating the space with your intentions.

In weaving crystals into the fabric of your home, you're doing more than just decorating; you're inviting an energy that transforms space, making it alive with possibility. Each crystal, carefully chosen and placed, becomes a beacon of the power you wish to cultivate, from the grounding presence of Hematite at your doorway to the dreamy caress of Moonstone by your bed. Your home, thus imbued with the essence of these earth treasures, becomes a living entity pulsating with the harmonious energy of the natural world.

Wearable Crystals: Jewelry and Accessories for Healing

In a world where every detail of our attire can reflect our inner selves, crystal jewelry stands out not just as an ornament but as a talisman, a source of energy we choose to carry close to our skin. This choice isn't merely about aesthetics; it's a deliberate act of aligning our external presence with our internal intentions. When we adorn ourselves with crystals, we weave their vibrational frequencies into the fabric of our daily lives, offering constant support for health, protection, and emotional balance.

Choosing Crystals for Daily Wear

Selecting crystal jewelry for the day ahead is as much an intuitive practice as it is a conscious decision. On mornings filled with anticipation of challenging tasks, a bracelet of Tiger's Eye can serve as a reminder of inner strength and resilience. A touch of Rose Quartz around the neck invites love and fosters connections for days that promise joy and social gatherings. This daily selection ritual allows us to pause and reflect on our needs, setting the tone for the day with intention and purpose.

- **Consider the day's activities**: Match your crystal to the day's potential stressors or joys. Lapis Lazuli can be your voice during presentations, while Black Tourmaline guards against negativity in crowded spaces.
- **Listen to your intuition**: Sometimes, a particular crystal might catch your eye or feel 'right' for no apparent reason. Trust these instincts; your body knows what energy it seeks.

Cleansing and Programming Jewelry

To ensure the crystals we wear continue to serve us with their most entire energy, regular cleansing, and programming become vital rituals. Just as we cleanse our bodies of the day's toils, our crystal jewelry, too, needs purifying from absorbed energies. A simple rinse under cool water or a night's rest on a Selenite plate can revive its vibrancy. Programming, or setting intentions, imbues the crystal with a specific purpose. Holding your Rose Quartz necklace in hand and whispering intentions of love and self-acceptance charges it with a focused energy, transforming it into a powerful ally.

- **Moonlight cleanse**: Once a month, under the glow of the full moon, lay your crystal jewelry out to bathe in its light. This celestial energy recharges the crystals, infusing them with renewed purpose.
- **Smoke cleanse**: Pass your jewelry through the smoke of sage or palo santo. This ancient practice clears negative energies, making way for your intentions to take hold.

Layering Crystals for Synergistic Effects

The art of layering crystal jewelry is a fashion statement and a strategic approach to amplifying healing effects. By combining different crystals, we can create a symphony of vibrations that work harmoniously to support multiple facets of our well-being. A necklace of Amethyst for peace layered with a Citrine bracelet for happiness crafts an aura of balanced energy. Each crystal's unique frequency enhances the other's properties, creating a cocoon of supportive energy around us.

- **Balance opposites**: Combine grounding stones like Hematite with uplifting stones like Citrine to maintain emotional equilibrium.
- **Enhance a single intention**: For focused energy on love, wear Rose Quartz with Rhodonite to amplify the heart's vibrations.

Crystal Accessories Beyond Jewelry

The realm of wearable crystals extends beyond the traditional confines of jewelry. The market now offers an array of crystal-embedded items that allow continuous energetic support in discreet or innovative ways.

- **Keychains and pins**: Attach a crystal keychain to your bag or a crystal pin to your jacket. These accessories serve as subtle reminders of your intentions and provide energetic support as you move through your day.
- **Crystal-embedded clothing**: Designers are increasingly incorporating crystals into clothing, from embroidery with small stones to pockets designed to hold crystals close to the body. This integration allows for a seamless blend of style and spirituality.
- **Customized crystal accessories**: Many artisans offer services to embed crystals into personal items like phone cases or bookmarks. This customization ensures that your daily tools also serve as sources of energy and intention.

Incorporating crystals into our attire and accessories does more than add a touch of nature's beauty to our appearance. It allows us to carry a piece of the earth's energy, a constant source of support and healing. As we move through our day, these crystals serve as silent allies, grounding us when we drift, uplifting us when we falter, and protecting us from the unseen tumults of the world. They remind us of our connection to the earth and the vast well of strength that lies within, waiting to be tapped. Through mindful selection, cleansing, and programming, our crystal jewelry becomes more than adornment; it becomes a tool for transformation and healing woven into our daily lives.

Crystals at Work: Enhancing Productivity and Focus

In the hum of the modern workplace, where deadlines loom, and creativity often finds itself under siege by stress, the subtle yet profound energies of crystals offer a sanctuary. They provide physical beauty to our workspaces and act as catalysts for focus, innovation, and calm. In the dance of day-to-day tasks, these stones whisper reminders of our deeper connections to the earth and our inner selves, fostering an environment where productivity and peace coexist.

Desk Crystals for Focus and Clarity

At the heart of every workspace, amidst the clutter of papers and the glow of computer screens, crystals like Fluorite and Tiger's Eye can stand as pillars of clarity and concentration. With its spectrum of colors, Fluorite acts as a mental cleanser, wiping away cluttered thoughts and fostering order. Tiger's Eye, on the other hand, sharpens our focus, its golden bands a beacon of determination and resolve. Together, they create a synergy, turning our desks into hubs of productivity:

- Place a piece of Fluorite next to your computer or notebook as a visual and energetic reminder to maintain focus.
- A Tiger's Eye paperweight can serve not just a practical purpose but as a talisman for strength and perseverance through challenging tasks.

Crystals for Stress Relief

Navigating work stress requires tools that address the mind and soothe the spirit. Lepidolite and Blue Lace Agate emerge as gentle allies in this endeavor. Lepidolite, rich in lithium, is calming, and its lavender hues are a visual balm for frazzled nerves. With its soft, serene patterns, Blue Lace Agate acts as a cooling touch on heated emotions, reminding us to breathe and center. Incorporating these crystals into our work environment can transform it into a space of tranquility:

- A small bowl of Lepidolite stones on your desk can be a reservoir of calm, inviting you to pause and reset when overwhelm threatens.
- Wearing a Blue Lace Agate bracelet or having a piece nearby during video calls can help keep communication smooth and stress at bay.

Crystals for Creativity and Communication

Innovation thrives not in solitude but in the spark of exchange. Carnelian and Blue Apatite serve as conduits for this creative fire and clarity in communication. Carnelian's vibrant orange stimulates the Sacral Chakra, the seat of creativity, encouraging bold ideas and the courage to bring them to life. Blue Apatite, mirroring the clarity of tropical waters, enhances our ability to articulate thoughts and fosters open dialogue. Their presence invites a flow of ideas, free from the barriers of doubt or hesitation:

- Keep a Carnelian stone in your pocket during brainstorming sessions as a source of inspiration and motivation.
- Place Blue Apatite on your desk or wear it as a necklace during presentations and meetings to aid in clear, confident communication.

Maintaining a Discreet Crystal Presence

For those in environments less open to the idea of crystals as work allies, subtlety becomes critical. Tiny, discreet crystals or crystal-infused items still offer personal support without drawing attention. A discreet piece of jewelry, a crystal-embedded pen, or even a keychain tucked away in a drawer allows you to benefit from the stones' energies without necessarily sharing your practice with the world:

- A small, polished stone like Hematite or Black Tourmaline can sit hidden under monitors or inside desk drawers, grounding and protecting without being in direct view.
- Crystal-infused stationery, like notepads with embedded stones, offers a way to draw upon crystal energy with every note taken or idea jotted down.

In the realm of work, where the tangible meets the intangible, crystals bridge worlds. They remind us that a deeper river of energy and intention lies beneath the surface of tasks and responsibilities. By inviting these stones into our workspaces, we enhance our productivity and focus and reconnect with the elemental forces that ground and guide us. This practice, subtle yet profound, transforms work into a ritual, infusing our daily tasks with meaning and our professional journey with a sense of harmony and purpose.

Traveling with Crystals: Protection and Peace on the Go

In the tapestry of life, travel stitches together moments of discovery, adventure, and, sometimes, the unexpected. Amidst the thrill of new landscapes and the rhythm of moving trains, planes, and bustling cities, our energy fields encounter diverse vibrations, not all contributing to our well-being. Here, crystals emerge as invaluable companions, safeguarding our energy and ensuring peace remains our constant travel mate.

Crystals for Travel Protection

Navigating through crowded airports or exploring unfamiliar streets, travelers seek not just physical safety but also protection from unseen energies. With its profound grounding properties, Black Tourmaline acts like a shield, absorbing negative frequencies and ensuring they don't attach to us. For those venturing into nature, Smoky Quartz offers an additional layer of defense, grounding us deeply to the earth and warding off environmental stressors.

- Carry a piece of Black Tourmaline in your pocket or luggage as a guardian against electromagnetic frequencies and negativity.
- A Smoky Quartz pendant keeps you connected to the earth's stabilizing energies, especially useful in preventing the disorientation of jet lag.

Crystals for Travel Anxiety

The anticipation of travel can stir a whirlpool of emotions, from excitement to an undercurrent of anxiety. In these moments, crystals serve as anchors, bringing calm to the heart and clarity to the mind. With its soothing oceanic hues, Aquamarine reminds us of the fluidity of experiences, encouraging adaptability and serenity. With its celestial connection, Angelite wraps us in a blanket of peace, facilitating angelic guidance on our journey.

- Before leaving, meditate with Aquamarine, visualizing your path ahead filled with ease and grace.
- Keeping an Angelite stone in your carry-on invites tranquility, ensuring your travels are enveloped in calm.

Packing Crystals for Travel

As we prepare for journeys, how we pack our crystalline allies matters as much as their selection. Ensuring their physical and energetic integrity is paramount, for a well-cared-for crystal radiates more robust protection and support.

- Wrap each crystal separately in a soft cloth or place them in a padded pouch to prevent chipping or energetic interference from other items.
- For air travel, consider placing your crystals in your carry-on luggage to keep their protective energy close and mitigate the stress of flying.

Creating a Portable Crystal Kit

A thoughtfully assembled travel crystal kit becomes a portable sanctuary, a reminder that no matter where we roam, our connection to the earth and its healing powers remains unbroken. Tailoring this kit to your travel needs infuses your journey with intention and care.

- **Grounding Stone**: A small Hematite or Red Jasper can keep you grounded, especially beneficial when crossing time zones.
- **Protection Stone**: Black Tourmaline or Smoky Quartz for safeguarding your energy in crowded or unfamiliar places.
- **Peace Stone**: Aquamarine or Angelite to maintain inner peace and navigate travel hiccups with grace.
- **Energy Stone**: Citrine or Sunstone invigorates after long hours of travel, keeping spirits high and fatigue at bay.

Place these stones in a silk or cotton pouch and bless them with a travel protection mantra or prayer before you set off. This consecration aligns their energies with your intentions, creating an invisible web of support around you.

Travel, in its essence, is an act of faith—a step into the unknown, trusting we'll find pieces of ourselves along the way. Crystals, our steady companions on this journey, ensure that no matter how far we wander, we remain tethered to the grounding and protective energies of the earth. They remind us that every journey, inward or across continents, is an opportunity for growth, protected and guided by the timeless wisdom of the natural world.

Chapter 6: Tailoring Crystals to Healing to Senior Needs

Imagine a tapestry woven from threads of wisdom, each strand representing a year in the rich tapestry of life. With age, this tapestry becomes more intricate, reflecting the beauty of experience but also the wear of time. This chapter explores how crystal healing can mend and strengthen these threads, explicitly focusing on bone health, a concern many faces as the years pass.

Crystals for Bone Health and Density Improvement

As the calendar pages turn, bones can become more fragile, a silent testament to the stories we've lived. Osteoporosis, a condition where bones lose their density, becomes a whisper in the lives of many seniors, echoing concerns of fragility. Yet, amidst these whispers, Calcite emerges as a beacon of strength, believed to support bone health and density.

- **Calcite for Bone Strength** Calcite, a crystal as robust as it is beautiful, stands out for its association with bone health. Imagine holding a piece of Calcite, its surface smooth yet solid, a tangible representation of strength. In the same way, Calcite is thought to support our skeletal system, offering its strength to our bones. This mineral, abundant in its variety, mirrors the body's natural composition, containing calcium, a fundamental building block of bone health.
- **Integrating Bone Health Crystals into Daily Life** Incorporating Calcite into daily routines doesn't require grand gestures. Simple acts, like placing a piece of Calcite on a windowsill where you enjoy your morning coffee, can serve as a quiet reminder of your intention for stronger bones. Wearing Calcite as a piece of jewelry not only keeps its supportive energy close but also adds a touch of earth's beauty to your day.
- **Complementary Practices** While crystals offer their support, they shine brightest as part of a chorus of healthy habits. Consider these practices as partners to your crystal healing:
    - **Dietary Considerations**: Foods rich in calcium and vitamin D are like best friends to your bones. Leafy greens, dairy products, and fish like salmon play supportive roles in your bone health symphony.
    - **Gentle Exercise**: Activities such as walking, tai chi, or gentle yoga encourage mobility and strength without overburdening fragile bones.

- **Sunlight**: Just like plants, we need sunlight to flourish. A daily dose of sunshine helps our body synthesize vitamin D, crucial for calcium absorption.

In this chapter, crystal healing reaches into the realm of practical, daily support, addressing specific needs that come with the wisdom of age. With its sturdy structure and composition mirroring our bones, Calcite offers a model for how the natural world can support our physical well-being. Through simple practices, thoughtful integration, and an awareness of complementary habits, crystal healing becomes a tangible part of nurturing the body's resilience, allowing the tapestry of our lives to remain vibrant and vital.

Enhancing Digestive Health with Crystals

The golden years bring a tapestry of changes, not least how our digestive system communicates with us. It begins to speak in more hushed tones, sometimes whispering of discomforts that were once foreign. This subtle shift impacts our physical health and enjoyment of life's simple pleasures, such as food and fellowship. In this light, the pursuit of digestive harmony becomes a quest for comfort, vitality, and joy.

Citrine for Digestive Support

Citrine emerges as a beacon of warmth and well-being in the realm of crystalline allies. Imagine this stone as a drop of sunlight captured forever in solid form, its energy reminiscent of a cozy, digestif-laden afternoon. Known for its bright, energizing presence, Citrine is reputed to spark the digestive fire, aiding in the breakdown and assimilation of nutrients. At the same time, it's sunny disposition may gently soothe stomach issues.

- **A Solar Companion**: Keeping Citrine close during meals, perhaps as a centerpiece or a piece of jewelry, invites its warm, supportive energy into the act of nourishment, making each bite an opportunity for healing.
- **Digestive Meditation**: Holding a piece of Citrine during meditation focuses the mind on the solar plexus chakra, the energy center tied to our digestive system. Visualize its golden light dissolving any discomfort, enhancing the body's natural healing capabilities.

Balancing Diet with Crystal Energy

The symphony of wellness is most harmonious when dietary wisdom accompanies crystal support. Introducing foods known for their digestive benefits while engaging with Citrine creates a duet of health-enhancing energies.

- **Fiber-Rich Foods**: Incorporate a variety of fruits, vegetables, and whole grains into your diet. These natural allies work with Citrine's energy to smooth the digestive process and maintain regularity.
- **Hydration and Herbal Teas**: Drinking plenty of water and soothing teas like ginger or peppermint aligns with Citrine's cleansing energy, further supporting digestive health.
- **Mindful Eating Practices**: Eating slowly and with gratitude, savoring each bite, amplifies the positive energy of the meal and Citrine alike, encouraging a peaceful digestive experience.

In this chapter, we've woven a narrative that positions Citrine as a luminary in the quest for digestive health, its golden light a constant companion in our days. Through practical applications and the harmonious blend of dietary wisdom, we invite a dance of vitality and joy into our golden years, transforming everyday nourishment into a celebration of life's abundance.

The partnership between crystal energy and mindful nutrition opens a pathway to enhanced well-being, where each meal becomes an opportunity for healing, and every moment of rest is a step toward vitality.

Crystals for Heart Health and Circulation

In the golden years of life, the heart, our most diligent and steadfast companion, begins to whisper of its need for a bit more care. The statistics around heart health issues in seniors paint a picture that cannot be ignored: the essence of vitality and longevity is so closely linked to how well this vital organ and its circulatory comrades perform their ceaseless dance. It's here, in the rhythm of our very lifeblood, that Rose Quartz steps in, a stone of gentle strength and profound healing, offering its support to heart health and emotional well-being.

Rose Quartz for Heart Health

Imagine Rose Quartz, with its soft pink hues, as a droplet of dawn's first light - promising, nurturing, and endlessly warm. This stone, revered across ages and cultures, is believed to cradle the heart in its soothing energies, supporting the physical organ and the wellspring of emotion and connection it symbolizes. Rose Quartz is like a balm for the heart's ailments, encouraging proper circulation and imbuing the whole system with peace and well-being.

Incorporating this stone into daily routines becomes an act of loving kindness towards oneself. Here are a few suggestions:

- **Wearing Rose Quartz**: Adorning oneself with Rose Quartz jewelry, especially pieces that rest near the heart, serves as a constant infusion of its healing energy. Whether it's a necklace, pendant, or brooch, the proximity to the heart center allows for a direct resonance, supporting cardiovascular functions and fostering emotional equilibrium.
- **Meditative Practices with Rose Quartz**: Holding a piece of Rose Quartz during meditation can deepen the practice, turning focus inward to the heart space. Visualize its tender pink light enveloping the heart, dissolving any blockages or discomfort, and promoting a healthy flow of energy throughout the body.

Complementary Cardiovascular Activities

The journey towards heart health is multifaceted, with Rose Quartz supporting a broader symphony of activities designed to keep the heart happy and healthy. Here are a few heart-healthy practices that pair beautifully with Rose Quartz's healing energy:

- **Gentle Exercise**: Activities such as walking, swimming, or light aerobics encourage cardiovascular fitness without straining the heart. Before starting, hold your Rose Quartz, setting an intention for a safe and nurturing workout. Post-exercise, reflect on the activity with the stone in hand, acknowledging your efforts towards heart health.
- **Heart-Healthy Diet**: A diet rich in omega-3 fatty acids, fiber, and antioxidants supports heart health. Consider placing a piece of Rose Quartz in the kitchen as a loving reminder to choose foods that nourish the heart. You might also create a small ritual before meals, holding the stone to infuse your food with positive, heart-supportive energy.
- **Relaxation and Stress Management**: Chronic stress can take a toll on heart health. Practices such as deep breathing, yoga, or tai chi not only reduce stress but also improve circulation. Integrating Rose Quartz into these practices, perhaps by creating a dedicated space with the stone present, amplifies the heart-healing intentions, making each session an act of self-care.

Visual Element: Journaling Prompts

Consider these guided journaling prompts to deepen the connection with Rose Quartz and its benefits for heart health. Keep your Rose Quartz nearby as you write, allowing its energy to inspire clarity and emotional release:

- Reflect on what your heart is truly seeking at this stage in your life. How can Rose Quartz support these desires?
- Write about any emotional blockages you feel may be impacting your heart health. Visualize Rose Quartz's light dissolving these barriers.
- Detail a daily routine that incorporates heart-healthy activities and Rose Quartz. How does this routine make you feel?

In the narrative of our lives, where each chapter builds upon the last, turning to the wisdom of crystals like Rose Quartz offers a way to support the heart's health and emotional well-being gently. It's a practice that acknowledges the intertwined nature of physical and emotional health, especially poignant in our later years. Through wearable tokens, meditative practices, and complementary activities, Rose Quartz becomes not just a stone but a steadfast companion on the journey towards heart-centered living. Its presence is a gentle reminder of the capacity for healing, the potential for peace, and the power of love.

Supporting Respiratory Health with Crystal Energy

In the quiet moments of reflection, we often find our thoughts turning toward the simple act of breathing, an automatic dance of life that sustains us from moment to moment. Yet, as the years gather, this effortless dance can become labored, a reminder of the essential need to nurture our respiratory health. Among seniors, concerns such as reduced lung capacity and the heightened risk of respiratory ailments underscore the importance of maintaining a healthy breath of life.

In this light, the Eucalyptus stone steps forward as a natural ally with its minty hues and refreshing essence. Named for its aromatic counterpart, the Eucalyptus tree, known for its decongestant properties, this stone is believed to carry with it the breath of the forest, offering support to the respiratory system and infusing the air with a vibrancy that mirrors the life-giving oxygen it helps us to assimilate.

Eucalyptus Stone for Respiratory Support

Imagine for a moment the cool, crisp air of an Eucalyptus grove, each breath a renewal; each exhales a release of the old. The Eucalyptus stone embodies this cycle, its energy purported to aid in clearing the respiratory pathways, supporting the lungs' vital function. It serves not just as a physical aid but as a reminder of the cleansing power of nature, of the body's inherent capacity to heal and rejuvenate itself.

- **Placement in Living Spaces**: Introducing Eucalyptus stone into your home environment, especially in areas where you spend much of your time, can transform the space into a haven of respiratory health. Consider placing a piece near your bed to promote clear breathing during sleep or in the living room to enhance air quality and energy flow.
- **Carrying Eucalyptus Stone**: Keeping a small Eucalyptus stone in a pocket or as a pendant ensures that its supportive energy is always close, acting as a personal shield

against environmental pollutants and aiding in maintaining respiratory clarity throughout the day.

Breathing Exercises with Eucalyptus Stone

Pairing the Eucalyptus stone with specific breathing exercises can amplify the benefits for respiratory health, creating a powerful practice for enhancing lung capacity and promoting ease of breath.

- **Deep Breathing Practice**: Holding a Eucalyptus stone, sit comfortably and close your eyes. Inhale deeply through the nose, imagining the stone's energy filling your lungs with refreshing, clean air. Hold your breath for a few seconds, then exhale slowly through the mouth, visualizing any respiratory blockages being released. Repeat this cycle for several minutes, allowing the stone's energy to work in harmony with your body's natural rhythms.
- **Guided Visualization**: With a Eucalyptus stone in hand, visualize yourself standing in a vast Eucalyptus Forest. With each inhale, draw in the forest's healing essence, feeling it cleanse and invigorate your respiratory system. With each exhale, release any heaviness or discomfort, letting the forest's energy carry it away.

Creating a Respiratory-Healthy Environment

Beyond personal practices, the Eucalyptus stone can also help create an environment that supports respiratory health. Its presence is a constant source of revitalizing energy, reminding us of the importance of clean air and our surroundings' role in our overall well-being.

- **Placement for Air Purification**: Position Eucalyptus stones around air purifiers, plants, or windows to encourage the circulation of clean, healthful air. Their energy can enhance the natural air-cleaning properties of plants and purifiers, creating a living space that supports respiratory health.
- **Creating a Respiratory Health Corner**: Dedicate a small area of your home as a respiratory health corner. Arrange Eucalyptus stones with other respiratory-supportive elements such as Himalayan salt lamps, air-purifying plants, and essential oil diffusers loaded with eucalyptus or peppermint oil. This space can serve as a retreat for deep breathing exercises, meditation, or simply a place to rest and enjoy the benefits of the purified air.

In the tapestry of our golden years, each thread represents a moment, a memory, a breath that has carried us to where we stand today. With its refreshing energy and supportive qualities, the Eucalyptus stone becomes a cherished companion on this journey, reminding us of the simple yet profound act of breathing deeply. Through its presence in our lives, from the spaces we inhabit to the practices we engage in, we find a renewed appreciation for each breath, each moment of clarity, and the infinite cycles of renewal that sustain us.

Crystals for Boosting Immune System in Seniors

As the seasons of life turn, bringing with them the wisdom and grace of senior years, our bodies whisper of the need for a little extra care, a touch more support. The immune system, that diligent sentinel, begins to signal its need for bolstering, a reminder that vitality remains a priority. In the quiet dialogue between body and spirit, it is here that Amethyst steps forward, a crystal of protection and purification, offering its energies to fortify the immune system.

Amethyst for Immune Strength

In the palette of healing crystals, Amethyst shines with a luminosity that transcends its physical beauty. Picture it: a stone of deep purples and soothing energies revered for its ability to calm the mind and its believed properties to enhance immune function. With its connection to the higher realms, this gem acts as a guardian against illness, purifying the body's energy field and enhancing its natural defenses.

Incorporating Amethyst into daily life becomes an act of nurturing, a subtle yet profound way to support the body's immunity.

- **Placing Amethyst in Living Areas**: By situating Amethyst around your home, particularly in spaces where relaxation and rejuvenation occur, you invite its purifying energy into your daily environment. This could mean a piece on the nightstand to oversee your rest, or a cluster in the living room, safeguarding the heart of your home.
- **Amethyst Jewelry for Continuous Support**: Wearing Amethyst as a piece of jewelry—a pendant, perhaps, that rests close to the heart—serves as a constant source of its protective energies. Not only does it adorn the body, but it also acts as a personal shield, safeguarding your well-being as you move through the day.
- **Meditative Practices with Amethyst**: Engaging in regular meditation with Amethyst can enhance its immune-boosting properties. Holding the stone or placing it before you as you meditate focuses the intention on health and vitality, aligning the body's energies for optimal wellness.

Lifestyle Factors for Immune Health

While Amethyst offers its support, it shines brightest when accompanied by lifestyle choices that foster immune health. These practices, woven into the fabric of daily life, create a holistic approach to maintaining vitality in senior years.

- **Nourishing Foods**: A diet rich in fruits, vegetables, and whole grains feeds not only the body but also the spirit. Foods high in antioxidants and vitamins support immune health at a cellular level. As you prepare meals, consider the presence of Amethyst in your kitchen as a visual reminder to choose foods that nourish your immune system.
- **Regular, Gentle Exercise**: Physical activity, tailored to your body's needs and abilities, can significantly enhance immunity. Activities like walking, stretching, or tai chi, done in the presence of Amethyst—perhaps a small stone in your pocket—marry movement with intention, strengthening the body and spirit.
- **Adequate Rest and Stress Management**: Quality sleep and stress reduction are pillars of immune health. Practices such as guided relaxation or gentle yoga before bed, especially with Amethyst nearby, encourage a deep, restorative sleep and a calm, centered mind.
- **Hydration and Herbal Teas**: Keeping the body well-hydrated is essential for immune function. Drinking plenty of water, perhaps from a glass infused with Amethyst's energy, ensures hydration while adding a layer of immune support. Herbal teas, especially those with echinacea or elderberry, complement Amethyst's properties and offer warmth and wellness in every cup.

In the dance of life, where each step carries the weight and wisdom of years lived, supporting the immune system becomes a melody of actions and intentions, a harmony of choices that nurture body and spirit. With its protective and purifying energies, Amethyst offers a chord in this melody, a note that resonates with the desire for health and vitality. Through its presence in our homes and lives, the mindful integration of supportive practices, and the embrace of a lifestyle that honors our well-being, we find a holistic approach to immune support. This approach, rooted in the wisdom of the earth and the knowledge of the self, carries us gracefully through the seasons of life, ensuring that each moment is lived with health, vitality, and a spirit that remains undimmed.

Managing Blood Pressure with Healing Stones

In the golden tapestry of life's later years, the whispering winds of change bring about shifts that touch upon the very core of our well-being. Among these, the rhythm and flow of our lifeblood, our blood pressure, calls for gentle yet vigilant care. With time, monitoring and managing blood pressure elevates, becoming crucial to maintaining health and vitality.

Bloodstone for Blood Pressure Regulation

In the realm of healing stones, Bloodstone emerges as a steadfast ally, its rich, verdant hues flecked with touches of crimson, a mirror to the life force it seeks to balance. Known since ancient times for its powerful connection to blood health, Bloodstone is revered not only for its fortifying energies but also for its believed ability to regulate and stabilize blood pressure.

The stone's grounding contributes to a sense of calm and balance, which is essential to managing blood pressure. It is a reminder of the strength and resilience within, encouraging a flow of energy supporting the body's natural rhythms and systems.

Daily Practices with Bloodstone

Integrating Bloodstone into the fabric of everyday life creates a grounding routine that supports blood pressure management. These daily practices become small acts of self-care, weaving the stone's stabilizing energies into the narrative of our days.

- **Carrying Bloodstone**: Keeping a piece of Bloodstone close, in a pocket or as a piece of jewelry, allows its energies to mingle with your own throughout the day, offering a constant, stabilizing influence on your blood pressure.
- **Bloodstone in Meditation**: Incorporating Bloodstone into meditation practices focuses intention on health and equilibrium. Holding the stone or placing it in front of you, visualize its grounding energy spreading through your body, soothing and balancing your blood pressure.
- **Placing Bloodstone for Sleep**: Positioning a Bloodstone near your bed or under your pillow as you sleep invites calm, restorative energies to work in tandem with your body's own healing processes during rest. This practice supports a relaxed state that is beneficial for blood pressure regulation.

Holistic Approach to Blood Pressure Management

While Bloodstone's supportive energies can help manage blood pressure, they shine brightest when part of a holistic approach that embraces lifestyle modifications aimed at heart health.

- **Balanced Diet**: A heart-healthy diet rich in fruits, vegetables, lean proteins, and whole grains supports not only overall health but specifically aids in maintaining optimal blood pressure levels. Foods high in potassium, magnesium, and calcium are especially beneficial, working in harmony with Bloodstone's energies.

- **Regular Exercise**: Engaging in regular physical activity, such as walking, cycling, or swimming, helps in maintaining a healthy blood pressure level. Start with gentle exercises, gradually increasing intensity as comfort and ability allow. Pairing exercise with Bloodstone enhances the grounding and energizing aspect of physical activity.
- **Stress Reduction Techniques**: Practices aimed at stress reduction, such as deep breathing, yoga, or tai chi, contribute significantly to blood pressure management. The calm induced by these activities, complemented by the stabilizing presence of Bloodstone, encourages a state of balance and well-being.
- **Adequate Hydration**: Keeping the body well-hydrated is essential for maintaining healthy blood pressure levels. Drinking water throughout the day, perhaps from a vessel that has been in the presence of Bloodstone, infuses hydration practices with the stone's supportive energies.

Incorporating Bloodstone into a lifestyle that values balanced nutrition, regular physical activity, stress management, and adequate hydration creates a comprehensive approach to managing blood pressure. This holistic method, grounded in the wisdom of ancient healing practices and modern wellness philosophies, offers a path to maintaining vitality and well-being in the golden years. Through the supportive energies of Bloodstone and mindful attention to lifestyle choices, the journey towards a balanced and healthy lifeblood unfolds, guided by the gentle hand of nature's gifts.

Crystals for Emotional Well-being and Loneliness

The golden years unfold with a depth of emotion and experience that paints daily in shades of joy, reflection, and, sometimes, solitude. In these moments of quiet, the heart yearns for connection, for the soft touch of compassion reminds us we're not alone. The tapestry of life, rich with its stories, also holds spaces of silence where loneliness whispers. Yet, within these spaces, a soothing presence comes from the earth - Lepidolite, a stone of emotional balance and comfort.

Lepidolite for Emotional Balance

Imagine the delicate layers of Lepidolite shimmering with the light of compassion and calm. With its soft lilac hues, this stone carries within it the serene energy of the evening sky, offering a sense of peace and emotional equilibrium. Lepidolite, rich in lithium, naturally embodies a stabilizing force, its presence a whisper of comfort to the soul experiencing loneliness or seeking emotional harmony.

In its embrace, stress dissolves, creating a tranquil heart and a soothed mind. Lepidolite doesn't erase the moments of solitude but transforms them into opportunities for reflection and growth, reminding us of the strength within stillness.

- **Wearing Lepidolite**: As a piece of jewelry, Lepidolite becomes a constant companion, its energy a subtle reminder of inner peace and resilience. A bracelet or pendant allows its calming influence to stay close, wrapping you in a blanket of comfort throughout the day.
- **Sleeping with Lepidolite**: Placing Lepidolite under your pillow or by your bedside invites gentle dreams and a restful sleep, its soothing vibrations a balm for the loneliness that often visits in the quiet of night.

Creating a Supportive Crystal Environment

The spaces we inhabit are reflections of our inner worlds, and with Lepidolite, they can become sanctuaries of emotional healing and connection. By integrating this stone into our living areas and personal meditation spaces, we create environments that not only nurture our well-being but also act as silent companions in moments of solitude.

- **Living Spaces**: A beautiful, raw piece of Lepidolite placed in common areas of the home serves as a visual and energetic focal point, radiating its calming energy throughout the space. It's a reminder that even in solitude, there's beauty and peace to be found.
- **Personal Meditation Spaces**: For those who have carved out a corner for reflection and meditation, adding Lepidolite to this space deepens the practice, its presence enhancing the sense of serenity and emotional release that meditation offers.

Activities to Complement Crystal Use

While crystals like Lepidolite offer their gentle support, engaging in activities that foster community and connection amplifies their benefits, creating a holistic approach to combating loneliness and nurturing emotional well-being.

- **Joining Community Groups**: Whether it's a book club, a gardening group, or a class at the local community center, participating in activities that interest you connects you with like-minded individuals, weaving new threads of friendship and support into the fabric of your life. Bringing along a piece of Lepidolite to these gatherings can serve as a personal anchor, keeping you centered and open in social settings.
- **Volunteer Work**: Offering your time and energy to causes you care about not only fills the heart but also builds bridges between souls. The act of giving, supported by the stabilizing energy of Lepidolite, reinforces the interconnectedness of all beings, reminding us that in giving, we receive.
- **Creative Expression**: Engaging in creative activities such as painting, writing, or crafting allows for emotional expression and exploration. Incorporating Lepidolite into your creative space can inspire tranquility and flow, turning moments of solitude into rich opportunities for self-expression and discovery.

In the dance of life's later years, where each step is an echo of the heart's journey, crystals like Lepidolite serve as beacons of light on the path. They remind us that within every moment of loneliness lies the potential for connection, within every wave of emotion, the possibility for peace. Through the thoughtful integration of Lepidolite into our daily lives, the creation of environments that nurture the soul, and the pursuit of activities that foster community and self-expression, we find a balanced approach to emotional well-being. This journey, supported by the gentle strength of Lepidolite, unfolds not in solitude but in the rich tapestry of shared human experience, where every heart finds its echo, and every soul, its song.

Enhancing Eye Health with Crystal Therapy

The golden years bring with them a treasure trove of memories and experiences, painting a rich tapestry of life lived in vibrant hues. However, as we navigate these years, maintaining the clarity and health of our eyes becomes paramount. Conditions such as macular degeneration and cataracts often cast shadows on this colorful journey, making tasks that once came easily—like reading a cherished book or admiring a sunset—a challenge. In this light, crystal therapy offers a gentle, supportive hand, guiding us towards practices that not only nurture our eye health but also enhance our connection to the world around us.

Aquamarine for Eye Health

Aquamarine, with its serene blue tones, mirrors the clarity of a tranquil sea, offering a reflection of health and rejuvenation for our eyes. This crystal, celebrated for its soothing properties, is believed to alleviate eye strain, and support the health of the visual system. Just as its name suggests, Aquamarine carries the essence of water—fluid, cleansing, and life-giving—making it an ideal companion for those seeking to support their eye health.

- **Meditation Focusing on Visual Health**: Integrating Aquamarine into meditation practices dedicated to eye health can be deeply beneficial. Holding the crystal or placing it before you, visualize its calming blue light enveloping your eyes, soothing any discomfort, and enhancing clarity. This focused intention, supported by Aquamarine's gentle energy, invites healing and rejuvenation.
- **Placing Aquamarine Near Work or Reading Areas**: For those who spend considerable time engaged in activities that strain the eyes, such as reading or working at a computer, placing Aquamarine nearby can offer supportive energy. The crystal's presence serves as a subtle reminder to take moments of rest, to blink and look away, allowing the eyes to relax and refresh.

Combining Crystal Therapy with Eye Health Practices

Incorporating Aquamarine into a holistic approach to eye health amplifies the benefits of both traditional and alternative practices. This combination creates a comprehensive care routine that not only addresses immediate concerns but also nurtures long-term well-being.

- **Regular Eye Exercises**: Engaging in exercises designed to strengthen the eye muscles can significantly enhance visual health. Pair these practices with Aquamarine to infuse them with the crystal's soothing energy. For example, after completing a series of eye exercises, hold Aquamarine close, allowing its calming influence to deepen the relaxation and rejuvenation of the eye muscles.
- **Conscious Breaks During Screen Time**: In an age where screens are an integral part of daily life, taking conscious breaks to rest the eyes is crucial. Use Aquamarine as a physical marker for these breaks—place the crystal near your screen as a visual cue to pause every 20 minutes, investigate the distance, and allow your eyes to relax.
- **Hydration and Diet**: Maintaining adequate hydration is vital for eye health, as it supports the natural lubrication of the eyes. Similarly, a diet rich in vitamins A, C, and E, along with minerals like zinc and selenium, provides the nutrients necessary for maintaining visual acuity and overall eye health. Infuse your water with Aquamarine to remind you of the importance of hydration, and consider preparing meals with the crystal nearby, setting an intention for nourishment and clarity.
- **Regular Check-ups with Eye Health Professionals**: While crystal therapy offers supportive energy, regular consultations with eye health professionals ensure that any changes in vision or eye health are promptly addressed. Carrying Aquamarine to these appointments can serve as a source of calm and clarity, reinforcing the partnership between traditional medical care and alternative healing practices.

In weaving Aquamarine into the fabric of our daily lives, we embrace a practice that honors the significance of maintaining eye health in our senior years. This crystal, with its serene energy and affinity for clarity, becomes a gentle guardian of our visual well-being, enhancing our ability to engage with the world in all its vibrant detail. Through focused meditation, mindful placement, and the integration of crystal therapy with conventional eye health practices, we create a holistic approach that nurtures not only our eyes but our entire being, allowing us to see the beauty of life with renewed clarity and appreciation.

Crystals for Skin Rejuvenation and Health

The skin, our body's largest organ, tells the story of our lives - every smile, frown, and moment spent under the sun. As we age, these stories become more pronounced, etching themselves into our very being. The desire to maintain the skin's health and vitality grows stronger, becoming a reflection of our inner health and our connection to the world around us.

Jade for Skin Rejuvenation

In the realm of crystals, Jade stands out as a beacon of beauty and renewal. This stone, with its deep connection to ancient traditions of healing and beauty, brings with it the promise of revitalized skin. Revered for its cooling properties, Jade is like the touch of a gentle breeze on a warm day, believed to encourage lymphatic drainage, reduce puffiness, and support the skin's natural renewal processes. Its green hues, a symphony of the earth's vitality, mirror the life force it seeks to instill in every cell, promising a complexion that glows with health and vitality.

Incorporating Jade into Skin Care Routines

Integrating Jade into daily skin care routines infuses an element of mindful self-care, turning routine into ritual. Here are some ways to invite the rejuvenating energy of Jade into your regimen:

- **Jade Rollers**: The use of Jade rollers has seen a resurgence, combining ancient wisdom with modern skin care practices. Gently rolling Jade across the face not only supports lymphatic drainage but also encourages better absorption of serums and moisturizers, enhancing their efficacy.
- **Jade as a Cooling Agent**: After a day in the sun or when your skin feels in need of a calming touch, a cool piece of Jade placed on the skin can soothe irritation and reduce redness. Its natural coolness, even at room temperature, offers immediate relief and comfort.
- **Placing Jade in Areas Dedicated to Personal Care**: Creating a space where Jade pieces are visibly placed in your bathroom or vanity serves as a reminder of your commitment to nurturing your skin. This visual cue reinforces the importance of self-care and the role of natural elements in supporting beauty from the inside out.

Holistic Skin Care Approach

A holistic approach to skin care recognizes that true beauty comes from a balance of external treatments and internal health. The supportive energy of Jade, combined with lifestyle choices that nurture well-being, creates a foundation for radiant skin:

- **Hydration**: Keeping the body well-hydrated is crucial for maintaining the skin's elasticity and vitality. Drinking ample water throughout the day, perhaps from a glass that has been sitting next to a piece of Jade, infuses your hydration practices with the intention of skin health.
- **Nutrition**: A diet rich in antioxidants, omega-3 fatty acids, and vitamins supports the skin's ability to renew and protect itself. Foods like berries, nuts, and green leafy

vegetables, enjoyed in an environment where Jade is present, aligns your nutritional choices with the energy of renewal and health.
- **Mindful Relaxation**: Stress can have a noticeable impact on the skin, from accelerating the aging process to exacerbating conditions like acne or eczema. Practices such as meditation or gentle yoga, especially when done in the presence of Jade, encourage a state of relaxation that reflects on the skin. The calming energy of Jade, combined with stress-reducing activities, supports a complexion that is as peaceful as the mind and spirit.

In weaving Jade into the narrative of skin care, we engage with an ancient ally, inviting its timeless beauty and healing properties into our modern lives. This integration of Jade into daily practices, from the tactile pleasure of using a Jade roller to the mindful arrangement of Jade pieces in personal care spaces, transforms routine into a deeply nurturing ritual. Through this holistic approach that honors the connection between external care and internal health, we invite the skin to tell a new story - one of rejuvenation, vitality, and a radiant glow that mirrors the life force within.

Conclusion

As we come to the end of this shared journey through the world of crystal healing, I want to take a moment to reflect on the path we've walked together. From the initial steps of understanding the foundational principles of crystals and their energies, through the exploration of practical applications for daily health concerns, to venturing into the realms of advanced techniques and ethical considerations in healing others, this journey has been one of discovery, growth, and transformation.

For you, the resilient women seniors who have walked this path with me, the exploration into the healing powers of crystals holds particular promise. The potential of these ancient stones to aid in improving sleep, rejuvenating memory, and alleviating arthritis is not just a testament to their versatility but a beacon of hope for enhancing holistic well-being. Remember, the integration of crystals into your daily routines, when approached with intention and mindfulness, can transform the mundane into the magical, elevating your quality of life in ways both subtle and profound.

It's important to underscore that while crystals are indeed powerful allies, their true effectiveness is unlocked by your intention, mindfulness, and commitment to your healing journey. These elements act as the soul of your practice, guiding and amplifying the energies of the crystals in alignment with your needs and aspirations.

Consider this book not as an end but as a gateway to a broader, more personal exploration of crystal healing. Your journey with crystals is deeply personal and ever-evolving. Trust in your intuition, allow your connection with these natural wonders to deepen, and be open to the insights and transformations they bring into your life.

Among the pages of this book, we've delved into budget-friendly crystals, offered a topical index for ease of use, and tailored our discussion to address the specific health concerns you face.

These features were designed with you in mind, aiming to empower you with knowledge and practical tools to embark on your healing journey confidently.

Now, I encourage you to take that first step, whether it's acquiring your first crystal, setting up a small crystal grid, or simply holding a crystal during meditation. Start where you are, with what you have, and let your curiosity and desire for well-being guide you.

I also invite you to share your journey with others. Connect with community groups, participate in online forums, or engage on social media to exchange stories, insights, and encouragement. There is strength in community, and your experiences can light the way for others just beginning their journey.

Remember, crystal healing is a deeply individual practice. Honor your unique pace, experiences, and emotions as you explore what works best for you. There is no right or wrong way, only what resonates with your body, mind, and spirit.

Lastly, I want to express my heartfelt gratitude for your trust and openness in exploring the healing potential of crystals. It's been an honor to guide you through these pages, and I hope you approach your practice with kindness, patience, and an ever-curious heart.

May your journey with crystals be filled with discovery, healing, and joy.

References

- *A Brief History of Crystals and Healing*
  https://www.crystalage.com/crystal_information/crystal_history/
- *Crystal healing: Stone-cold facts about gemstone treatments*
  https://www.livescience.com/40347-crystal-healing.html
- *Healing Crystals at Home: The Science Within*
  https://crystalshealing.co.uk/blogs/crystals-tips/healing-crystals-at-home
- *The Power of Healing Crystals: Personal Story*
  https://www.holisticdivineinnovations.org/blog/the-power-of-healing-crystals-personal-story
- *Insomnia in the Elderly: A Review - PMC*
  https://www.ncbi.nlm.nih.gov/pmc/articles/PMC5991956/
- *Crystals for Sleep: Catch More ZZZ's with These Healing ...*
  https://www.healthline.com/health/sleep/crystals-for-sleep
- *How to Create and Use a Crystal Grid (Step-by-Step)*
  https://loveandlightschool.com/how-to-create-use-a-crystal-grid-step-by-step/
- *Synchronization of human sleep with the moon cycle under ...*
  https://www.ncbi.nlm.nih.gov/pmc/articles/PMC7840136/

- *Memory Problems, Forgetfulness, and Aging* https://www.nia.nih.gov/health/memory-loss-and-forgetfulness/memory-problems-forgetfulness-and-aging
- *Clear Quartz Healing Properties - Charms Of Light* https://www.charmsoflight.com/clear-quartz-healing-properties#:~:text=Clear%20Quartz%20enhances%20psychic%20abilities,and%20aligns%20the%20subtle%20bodies.
- *5 Must Have Crystals For Senior Citizens* https://crystalagatebracelets.com/blogs/news/5-must-have-crystals-for-senior-citizens
- *Healing Crystals: Benefits, Uses And Where To Buy* https://www.forbes.com/health/wellness/guide-to-healing-crystals/
- *CRYSTALS, INFLAMMATION, AND OSTEOARTHRITIS* https://www.ncbi.nlm.nih.gov/pmc/articles/PMC3154781/
- *Healing Benefits of Wearing Copper and How to Care for ...* https://www.ivyandlight.com/blog-posts/how-to-care-for-copper-jewelry
- *Top 10 Cheapest Crystals For Beginners: Ultimate Guide ...* https://thespiritnomad.com/blog/cheapest-crystals/
- *8 Ways To Use Healing Crystals In Your Everyday Routine* https://www.mindbodygreen.com/articles/how-to-use-crystals-everyday
- *Healing Crystals: Benefits, Uses And Where To Buy* https://www.forbes.com/health/wellness/guide-to-healing-crystals/
- *Top 10 Cheapest Crystals For Beginners: Ultimate Guide ...* https://thespiritnomad.com/blog/cheapest-crystals/
- *How to Cleanse Crystals: 10 Ways, Plus Tips for Charging, ...* https://www.healthline.com/health/how-to-cleanse-crystals
- *Crystal healing: Stone-cold facts about gemstone treatments* https://www.livescience.com/40347-crystal-healing.html
- *Healing Crystals: Benefits, Uses And Where To Buy* https://www.forbes.com/health/wellness/guide-to-healing-crystals/
- *Calcite Meaning: Healing Properties & Everyday Uses* https://tinyrituals.co/blogs/tiny-rituals/calcite-meaning-healing-properties-everyday-uses
- *Crystal healing: Stone-cold facts about gemstone treatments* https://www.livescience.com/40347-crystal-healing.html
- *Crystals for Seniors - Healingcrystals.com* https://www.healingcrystals.com/Crystals_for_Seniors_Articles_16882.html
- *How to Create Crystal Elixirs Safely* https://loveandlightschool.com/create-crystal-elixirs-safely/
- *Crystal Grids: Complete Guide (Updated 2024)* https://www.healingcrystalsco.com/blogs/blog/crystal-grids-complete-guide
- *The Ultimate Guide to Using Crystals in Yoga and Meditation* https://michalandcompany.com/ultimate-guide-using-crystals-in-yoga-and-meditation/
- *Consent And Distant Energy Healing* https://www.blissfullight.com/blogs/energy-healing-blog/consent-and-distant-energy-healing

Printed in Great Britain
by Amazon